flourless.

RECIPES FOR NATURALLY GLUTEN-FREE DESSERTS

NICOLE SPIRIDAKIS | PHOTOGRAPHS BY JOHN LEE

CHRONICLE BOOKS

SAN FRANCISCO

Library of Congress
Cataloging-in-Publication
Data available.

ISBN 978-1-4521-1955-7

Manufactured in China

MIX
Paper from
responsible sources
FSC® C008047

Designed by River Jukes-Hudson
Food styling by Jeffrey Larsen
Prop styling by Ethel Brennan
Food styling assistance by Alexa Hyman
and Anne-Christina Milne

10 9 8 7 6 5 4 3 2 1

Chronicle Books LLC
680 Second Street
San Francisco, California 94107
www.chroniclebooks.com

To flourless bakers everywhere.
....
And to my family.

Introduction

Sometimes I dream in cake. I wake up with my fingertips tingling with the memory of assembling freshly baked pavlovas layered with whipped cream and berries, towering angel food cakes infused with citrus zest and sprinkled with poppy seeds, polenta cakes made just slightly tart by the addition of sour cream, strawberry-rhubarb cakes sweetened with maple syrup. I yawn my way into the kitchen and turn on the oven, still in a dream state, to make honeyed cornmeal-blueberry cakes for breakfast while sipping coffee to prop open my eyelids.

I wind a scarf around my shoulders to counter the inevitable morning chill that descends upon San Francisco even in summer and plot my day: a flourless chocolate cake with salted caramel sauce for a dinner party, a hazelnut cake draped with chocolate glaze for a birthday celebration. I clutch at the vague recollection of the dreamscape and come up with interesting flavor combinations for future projects—a Mexican hot chocolate—inspired chocolate cake made with ground oats and nutty flax seeds, its slight fire tamed by a cool swath of chocolate-buttermilk frosting, and to be made as soon as possible. I will wash a lot of dishes.

San Francisco, where I live, is a city of sea air and ships, salt and sourdough bread. During the more than half a decade I've called it home, I've come to embrace the fog that winds through my neighborhood each July without fail. To counter that summer coolness and to indulge my penchant for baked goods, I bake a lot. I bake for pleasure and for friends and family, but always to experiment.

The idea for this cookbook came after dinner on a frigid night in Maine while I was visiting my brother and sister-in-law. As Kurt did the washing up, Emily and I sat around the kitchen table with a plate of flourless almond cookies and tea, their cat, Fotis, begging for crumbs at our feet. The conversation turned to food and then to flourless baking specifically because Emily keeps to a gluten-free diet. As we talked, we explored the idea that it's often a bit easier to make desserts that did not call for any wheat flour at all compared to those that incorporated a gluten-free flour substitute. Thus the idea of naturally flourless—meaning desserts that are naturally wheat flour–free and unequivocally, objectively delicious regardless—was born.

When I returned home to my tiny California kitchen, I became quietly obsessed. I sought out cake recipes that were based on ground nuts, egg whites, a small amount of cornstarch. I roasted fruit and piled a delicious mixture of rolled oats and brown sugar atop berries. I baked creamy egg custards infused with bright citrus zest and a revelatory chocolate cake that contained not a teaspoon of all-purpose flour (and which was impossible to stop eating).

As I worked, I realized that there are so many flourless desserts that can be put together with easily accessible and inexpensive ingredients plus a fairly simple technique. I was also struck with a pang for all of those who don't have the option of easily obtaining sweets because of dietary restrictions or allergies (on my forays around town I

will admit to often blithely picking up a sweet treat here and there with nary a qualm). If you can't have gluten, going into a bakery can be a frustrating experience in denial. Likewise, baking at home can be fraught with complicated, expensive, or hard-to-obtain components.

This is the crux of *Flourless.*—recipes for unqualifiedly great desserts that do not call for hard-to-find ingredients and that also happen to be gluten-free—the naturally flourless concept made real. In this volume you will not find complicated gluten-free flour mixes or recipes calling for additional binders such as xanthan or guar gum. Instead, you will find instructions for naturally wheat flour–free desserts that will tempt even the most skeptical.

Flourless baking may seem daunting, but it needn't be. The main thing to keep in mind when creating flourless desserts is to not see them as substitutions for more traditional sweets (along the lines of: it's almost as good as x, y, or z). These desserts are delicious in their own right, regardless of whether or not they call for wheat flour.

Nuts, egg whites (and yolks, too), fresh fruit, and good chocolate are your allies here. Reliance on unfussy, straightforward flavors and those that work well together is your game plan. Think plums and pistachios, apples and cornmeal, chocolate and hazelnuts, coconut and lemon.

Don't be intimidated! Sure, we may be stepping a bit outside our comfort zone when avoiding recipes that call for wheat flour, but that doesn't mean we can't be bold. Embrace the grit of cornmeal. Experiment with walnuts. Become enamored of the magic that is whipped egg whites.

Here, you will not find any recipes calling for all-purpose flour but you will find recipes for a (delectable, rich but not too) milk chocolate pudding, lemon cream pie with a coconut-almond crust, meringue cookies, citrus-spiked flan, a myriad of simple candies, and so much more.

I hold myself to a high standard when baking and creating desserts; and when I do so without gluten, my intention is no different.

About Substitutions

I firmly believe that all good things are enjoyed best in moderation, and dessert is no exception. I also firmly believe in sharing desserts—especially the sort that are creamy and delicious and of which you really only need to eat just one piece. So you will find butter in this cookbook, and whole eggs, too, in addition to a decent amount of sugar.

At the same time, I've tried to provide some recipes that incorporate natural sweeteners such as maple syrup, honey, and fruit, as well as for some desserts that are generally a little on the lighter side. In short, I have aimed for balance—as essential in cooking as it is in life. There are also some simple substitutions to tailor these desserts for those who can't have dairy or eggs.

BUTTER SUBSTITUTE

Substitute the equivalent amount of nondairy margarine (such as Earth Balance) for butter in cookie recipes, particularly when it must be creamed. The same goes for cakes that call for butter; an oil of choice (such as coconut, olive, or vegetable oil) often is fine as well. Note that vegetable is a neutral oil, while coconut and olive have distinct flavors; all will work in these recipes, but you may want to choose your oil based on taste preferences.

COW'S MILK SUBSTITUTE

Substitute a nondairy milk, such as soy or almond milk, for milk, yogurt, or buttermilk. To make a buttermilk equivalent, stir 1 tsp of white vinegar into 1 cup/240 ml of nondairy milk and let sit for 5 minutes before using in the recipe. Or try coconut milk whipped cream (see page 136) in place of whipped cream in any of these recipes.

EGG SUBSTITUTE

When bread, cake, or cookie recipes call for eggs as a binder, substitute a flax "egg." Vigorously whisk 1 tbsp of flax meal into 3 tbsp of boiling water and let rest for at least 20 minutes before using. This is the equivalent of one whole egg.

In recipes in which egg whites act as a leavener, such as an angel food cake or macaron cookies, it is unfortunately not possible to use a substitute.

Making Your Own Wheat–Free Flours

NUT MEAL AND FLOUR

Grind nuts into nut meal yourself in a food processor, coffee mill, or coffee grinder (or a blender in a pinch) until a fine powdery meal forms. Watch carefully so you do not overgrind or the nuts may form a paste. Or use pre-ground nuts that you may find in your local grocery store. Almond flour, which is fairly easy to obtain, may be used in place of almond meal in all of the recipes; the texture of the resulting dessert will be a tad finer than if ground nuts are used but it will be no less good.

Nuts may be ground in advance of baking and stored in sealed mason jars in the freezer so the nut meal stays fresh and conveniently on hand.

OAT MEAL/FLOUR

You may substitute pre-made or store-bought oat flour for ground oats in any recipe in this book as follows: 1 cup/85 g rolled oats roughly equals 1 cup/90 g finely ground oats or oat flour.

HOW TO MEASURE INGREDIENTS

For the recipes in this cookbook it is best to scoop and then level the nut meals and other dry ingredients.

A few other cautions

If you are keeping to a gluten-free diet, particularly if you have celiac disease or are very allergic to gluten, seek out ingredients that are labeled "gluten-free" and use products with which you are familiar and that you know are safe for you to eat (including gluten-free oats, baking powder, baking soda, cornmeal, cornstarch, vanilla extract, etc.). It is assumed for the purposes of the recipes included in this cookbook that the ingredients called for are meant to be gluten-free.

If you are baking or cooking for someone who has a gluten allergy, take the proper steps to avoid cross-contamination. Use wooden spoons that are reserved solely for gluten-free baking or use non-wooden utensils, because gluten can become trapped in the wood fibers. The same goes for cutting boards. Make sure all implements that are also used for cooking with wheat flours, including bowls and measuring spoons and cups, are thoroughly washed before using them. Clean your cooking area very well so there is no chance a speck of gluten remains that can contaminate your flourless creation. Ask in advance if there are any specific products or ingredients that you should avoid so as to not trigger a reaction.

Cakes and Cupcakes

Last January, I went for a hike along the Northern California coast with a few old friends on a brilliant blue day full of sun and brisk wind, one of those days that makes you glad to be alive. When we came home, I served thick slices of chocolate cake made from ground oats and flax seeds and topped with a generous swath of brown sugar buttercream (see page 22). We drank tea and toasted our tired toes in front of the fire in a comfortable silence broken only by the scrape of a fork against a plate. It was a perfect afternoon. (I need hardly mention that the cake contained not a teaspoon of all-purpose flour.)

Now, I can't claim that a chocolate cake can create world peace, but I can argue that it can bring about happiness and contentment—at least for a few hours. Sinking a fork into a fluffy piece of cake and taking that first bite . . . this is the stuff of which dreams are made. Even better if those dreams happen to incorporate naturally flourless cake.

To achieve wonderful cakes without flour, it's helpful to rely upon egg whites for loft and the occasional inclusion of ground nuts for additional oomph. (Remember to bring your egg whites to room temperature for at least 20 minutes before using, as this will result in a higher volume when beaten.) Cornmeal, too, adds a lovely texture, particularly when paired with fresh fruit or citrus zest. In fact, fruit can elevate an ordinary flourless cake to the extraordinary, such as in a chocolate cake made delightful by scattering it with sliced pears (see page 25) or in a seemingly simple white cake, such as a rich almond cake topped with balsamic-roasted strawberries (see page 36).

In this chapter, you'll find a variety of cakes to suit every occasion, from a quick weeknight treat to an elegant dinner party: a maple syrup–sweetened strawberry-rhubarb cornmeal cake that fairly sings of spring, a pillowy angel food cake made airy with beaten egg whites and laced with poppy seeds, a coffee-drenched opera cake that incorporates a flourless almond sponge cake, small pistachio-plum beauties that are dairy-free as well as flourless. And cupcakes, too: tender white cupcakes capped with a swath of brisk lemon buttercream frosting and dense chocolate cupcakes topped with salted caramel frosting.

The only difficulty here may be in choosing which recipe to try first.

Flourless Chocolate Cake with Salted Caramel Sauce

SERVES 10

A solid recipe for a flourless chocolate cake should be in every cook's arsenal, and consequently there are many variations on a theme (the Gâteau Victoire at San Francisco's Zuni Café being a particular favorite of mine). Here, the flavors of hazelnuts, coffee, and good butter create a luscious undernote to the rich chocolate. Generously drizzle salted caramel sauce over each portion before serving.

FLOURLESS CHOCOLATE CAKE

2 oz/55 g bittersweet chocolate, chopped

¾ cup/170 g unsalted butter, cut into pieces

6 large eggs

1 cup/200 g packed dark brown sugar

¼ cup/60 ml strong brewed coffee

1½ cups/140 g ground hazelnuts

1 tsp salt

SALTED CARAMEL SAUCE

1 cup/100 g granulated sugar

¼ cup/60 ml water

4 tbsp/55 g unsalted butter, cut into pieces

¾ cup/180 ml heavy cream

1 tsp salt

To make the cake: Position the rack in the center of the oven and heat the oven to 350°F/180°C. Butter a 9-in/23-cm cake pan, and line the bottom with parchment paper. Wrap the outside of the pan tightly with three layers of heavy-duty aluminum foil.

In a medium metal bowl set over a saucepan of simmering water, combine the chocolate and butter, whisking until the mixture is melted and smooth. Remove the bowl from the pan.

In a large bowl, whisk the eggs, brown sugar, and coffee to blend. Add the melted chocolate mixture and whisk until smooth. Stir in the ground hazelnuts and salt. Transfer the batter to the prepared pan.

Place the pan in a large roasting pan. Pour enough hot water into the roasting pan to come halfway up the sides of the cake pan. Tent the cake pan loosely with foil and place the roasting pan in the oven.

Bake until the cake is set in the center when jiggled slightly and the top is dry to the touch, about 1½ hours (the top of the cake will remain shiny). Remove the cake pan from the roasting pan and discard the foil from the top and sides of the pan. Cool the cake in the pan on a wire rack, then chill until cold, about 3 hours.

While the cake is chilling, make the caramel sauce: Place the sugar and water in a medium saucepan and bring to a boil over medium-high heat, whisking until the sugar melts. Decrease the heat to medium and slowly boil, without whisking the mixture, until a deep amber caramel forms, about 6 minutes. Watch so the sugar does not burn.

Remove the saucepan from the heat and carefully whisk in the butter (it will foam up). Whisk in the cream (it will foam up again) and salt. Let the caramel cool to room temperature before using. The sauce will keep in a sealed container in the fridge for up to 2 weeks.

Use a serrated knife to cut the cake into thin wedges and drizzle them with the caramel sauce to serve.

Chocolate Cake with Brown Sugar Buttercream

SERVES 10

Tender, not-too-sweet, and a bit nutty from the ground oats, this dessert is just about everything you could wish for in a chocolate cake. When I served it to friends along with cups of strong tea as we sat in a little cabin in the woods, a contented silence reigned, broken only by the occasional bird's call and the crackle of the fire in the stove until the plates were scraped clean. Then we had seconds. Serve slices with scoops of vanilla ice cream, too. *Note: Flax seeds may be bought already ground or you may grind whole seeds in a coffee grinder until a fine meal forms.*

CHOCOLATE CAKE

1 tsp ground flax seeds

2 tsp boiling water

2 oz/60 g semisweet chocolate, melted and slightly cooled

¾ cup/180 ml vegetable oil

¾ cup/180 ml low-fat plain yogurt

3 large eggs, at room temperature

1 tsp pure vanilla extract

1 cup/200 g packed light or dark brown sugar

6 tbsp/20 g unsweetened cocoa powder

1½ cups/170 g ground oats

¼ tsp salt

1½ tsp baking powder

BROWN SUGAR BUTTERCREAM

½ cup/115 g unsalted butter,
at room temperature

¼ cup/50 g packed light or dark brown sugar

3 oz/85 g semisweet chocolate, melted

½ tsp pure vanilla extract

1 cup/100 g confectioners' sugar

2 to 3 tbsp whole milk, if necessary

To make the cake: Heat the oven to 350°F/180°C. Grease a 9-in/ 23-cm round baking pan and line with parchment paper.

In a small bowl, whisk the ground flax seeds with the boiling water to form a paste. Let rest for 10 minutes before using.

In a large bowl, whisk together the flax seed paste, melted chocolate, vegetable oil, yogurt, eggs, vanilla, and brown sugar. In a medium bowl, whisk together the cocoa powder, ground oats, salt, and baking powder. Add the dry mixture to the wet mixture and stir well to combine.

Pour the batter into the prepared pan and bake until the cake is firm and a tester inserted in the middle comes out clean, about 30 minutes.

Remove from the oven and let cool in the pan for 5 minutes, then turn out onto a wire rack and cool completely.

To make the buttercream: In a large bowl, using an electric mixer, cream the butter and brown sugar on medium-high. Add the chocolate and vanilla and beat well to combine. Add the confectioners' sugar and beat well until smooth. Add a little milk if the frosting seems too dry.

When ready to assemble, halve the 9-in/23-cm cake round horizontally to make two equal layers and spread the bottom layer with about one-third of the prepared buttercream. Place the remaining cake round on top and use the remaining buttercream to frost the sides and top of the cake. Alternatively, don't cut the cake in half and use all of the butter-cream to thickly frost the sides and top of the cake.

Cut the cake into generous slices to serve.

Pear-Chocolate Cake

SERVES 10

Sweet, juicy pears nestle into a pistachio-laden cake batter that puffs up
alluringly once baked. Each mouthful brings a wonderful blend
of fruit, chocolate, and nuts that's nearly irresistible. I serve this cake plain,
but whipped cream and chocolate sauce would be very nice if you like.

4 oz/115 g semisweet chocolate,
broken into pieces

6 tbsp/85 g unsalted butter

1 tsp pure vanilla extract

3 large eggs, separated

¾ cup/85 g sugar

⅔ cups/85 g ground pistachio nuts

4 ripe pears, peeled, cored, and quartered

Heat the oven to 350°F/180°C. Line the bottom of a 9-in/23-cm
springform pan with parchment paper and butter the paper and the
sides of the pan.

Melt the chocolate and butter in a metal bowl placed over a pan of simmering water. Remove from the heat, stir in the vanilla, and let cool.
In a large bowl, whisk the egg yolks with the sugar until pale and thick,
then fold in the melted chocolate mixture and the ground pistachios.

In another large bowl, beat the egg whites until they reach soft peaks
but are not dry. Stir a spoonful of the whites into the chocolate to lighten
the batter a bit, then carefully fold in the rest of the whites in two
additions until they are completely incorporated. Spoon the batter into
the prepared pan and smooth with a rubber spatula. Arrange the pears
over the top of the batter, cut-side down, in a circular pattern.

Bake until the pears are soft, the cake is cooked through, and a tester
inserted in the middle comes out clean, about 40 minutes. Remove from
the oven and cool in the pan on a wire rack for 10 minutes, then remove
the sides of the pan and place the cake on the rack to cool completely.

Cut the cake into wedges to serve.

Mexican Hot Chocolate Cake with Milk Chocolate–Buttermilk Frosting

SERVES 10

Traditional Mexican hot chocolate is marked by the addition of cinnamon and a pinch of ground dried chile, bringing a complexity that's sometimes lacking in a more ordinary mug. I'm not one for lots of hot spice—my husband makes a hot chocolate laced with cayenne pepper and brandy on rainy winter days that I can only sip at before wincing. But this cake, run through with cinnamon, gives enough kick to keep one's interest, while the milk chocolate–buttermilk frosting soothes any lingering angst. If the idea of a spicy cake is simply too odd, omit the cayenne. *Note: Flax seeds may be bought already ground or you may grind whole seeds in a coffee grinder until a fine meal forms.*

MEXICAN HOT CHOCOLATE CAKE

1 tsp ground flax seeds

2 tsp boiling water

¾ cup/180 ml vegetable oil

¾ cup/180 ml buttermilk

1 cup/200 g packed light or dark brown sugar

1 tsp pure vanilla extract

3 large eggs, at room temperature

1½ cups/170 g ground oats

6 tbsp/60 g unsweetened cocoa powder

1½ tsp baking powder

1 tbsp ground cinnamon

¼ tsp cayenne pepper

¼ tsp salt

continued

MILK CHOCOLATE–BUTTERMILK FROSTING
½ cup/115 g unsalted butter,
at room temperature

2 oz/60 g milk chocolate, melted

½ tsp pure vanilla extract

1 cup/100 g confectioners' sugar

2 to 3 tbsp buttermilk

To make the cake: Heat the oven to 350°F/180°C. Line the bottoms of two 8-in/20-cm or 9-in/23-cm round cake pans with parchment paper and lightly grease the paper and the sides of the pans with vegetable oil.

In a small bowl, whisk the ground flax seeds with the boiling water to form a paste. Let rest for 10 minutes before using.

In a large bowl, whisk together the flax seed paste, vegetable oil, buttermilk, brown sugar, vanilla, and eggs. In a medium bowl, whisk together the ground oats, cocoa powder, baking powder, cinnamon, cayenne, and salt. Add the dry mixture to the wet mixture to make a batter and stir well to combine.

Evenly divide the batter between the two prepared pans and bake until the cake tops are firm and shiny, about 30 minutes. Remove from the oven and let the cakes cool in the pans on a wire rack for 10 minutes before turning them out onto the rack to cool completely.

To make the frosting: Place the butter in a large bowl and beat with an electric mixer on medium speed until fluffy. Add the melted chocolate and vanilla and beat well to incorporate. Add the confectioners' sugar and 2 tbsp of the buttermilk and continue beating until a smooth, fluffy icing forms, about 5 minutes. Add a bit more buttermilk if the frosting seems too dry.

When ready to assemble, spread about half of the frosting on one of the cake rounds, then top with the other cake round and use the remaining frosting to thickly cover the top of the cake.

Cut the cake into thick wedges to serve.

Angel Food Cake

SERVES 12

The loft of an angel food cake comes from egg whites whipped until they are light and filled with air, with a bit of sugar and cornstarch folded in for substance. To make a plain angel food cake—or to make a flourless sponge cake—omit the poppy seeds and the fruit zest and juice called for here. Use egg whites that are at least 3 days old to achieve the best results and bring them to room temperature before whipping. Serve with whipped cream and fresh fruit if you like.

12 egg whites, at room temperature

1 tbsp fresh lemon juice

1 tbsp warm water

½ tsp salt

1¼ tsp cream of tartar

1 tsp pure vanilla extract

1¼ cups/250 g sugar

1 cup/110 g cornstarch

3 tbsp poppy seeds

Grated zest of
1 medium organic grapefruit, orange,
blood orange, or lemon, plus
1 tbsp of its juice

Heat the oven to 350°F/180°C.

In a large bowl, beat the egg whites, lemon juice, and warm water with an electric mixer on medium-high speed until foamy. Add the salt, cream of tartar, and vanilla and keep beating until the egg whites start to hold soft peaks.

Still beating, add 1 cup/200 g of the sugar, 1 tbsp at a time. The whites will become glossy and will hold firmer peaks; do not let them get too stiff.

continued

Sift together the remaining ¼ cup/50 g sugar with the cornstarch, then gently and quickly fold the mixture into the egg whites with a rubber spatula. Try to fully incorporate the cornstarch mixture into the whites while still keeping the loft of the whipped egg whites. Gently fold in the poppy seeds, citrus zest, and citrus juice.

Pour the batter into a clean, 12-cup/2.8-L tube pan and draw a thin spatula gently through the batter to eliminate any large air pockets. Bake until the cake is puffed and its surface is lightly browned and cracked, 45 to 55 minutes.

Remove the cake from the oven and invert the pan on a wire rack. Let the cake hang upside down for about 1½ hours (use a wine bottle to prop up the cake while it's inverted if your tube pan does not have "feet") until it is thoroughly set and cooled, then gently remove from the pan.

Using a large serrated knife, gently and quickly cut generous slices of cake to serve. Angel food cakes can compress easily, so the less handling while cutting, the better.

Coconut Cake with Chocolate Ganache Glaze

SERVES 8

The genius of this cake is in the strange magic that happens when flaked coconut is whirled with cornstarch and eggs (plus a few other ingredients) in the food processor. Though there's not a speck of flour called for, the cake's crumb is moist and delicate, the perfect bolster to a swath of dark chocolate ganache frosting.

COCONUT CAKE

2 cups/115 g unsweetened flaked coconut

⅔ cup/130 g sugar

½ cup/55 g cornstarch

3 large eggs, at room temperature

7 tbsp/100 g unsalted butter, cut into a few pieces, at room temperature

1 tsp pure vanilla extract

1¼ tsp baking powder

½ tsp salt

Grated zest of 1 organic lemon

CHOCOLATE GANACHE GLAZE

3 oz/85 g semisweet chocolate

½ cup/120 ml heavy cream

1 tbsp warm water

To make the cake: Heat the oven to 350°F/180°C. Line the bottom of an 8-in/20-cm round cake pan with parchment paper and butter the paper and sides of the pan.

Place the coconut, sugar, cornstarch, eggs, butter, vanilla, baking powder, salt, and lemon zest in the bowl of a food processor fitted with a steel blade. Process until a smooth batter forms, at least 1 minute. Pour into the prepared pan and bake until the cake is lightly browned, firm to the touch, and a tester inserted into the middle comes out clean, 30 to 35 minutes. Remove from the oven and cool on a wire rack in the pan for 10 minutes, then turn out onto the rack to cool completely.

To make the glaze: Place the chocolate in a bowl and set aside. Warm the cream on the stove until it is just below boiling. Pour the cream over the chocolate and let stand for 5 minutes, then whisk to combine. Whisk in the warm water and continue whisking until the chocolate is completely melted and the ganache is very smooth. Cool slightly to room temperature before using.

When ready to assemble, spread a thick layer of chocolate ganache over the top of the cooled cake. Let set for about 20 minutes until firm.

Cut the cake into medium-thick slices to serve. The cake may be stored in an airtight container at room temperature for up to 2 days.

Hazelnut Cake with Salted Chocolate Glaze

SERVES 10

Hazelnut paste is quite easy to make: combine hazelnuts with sugar and egg whites in a food processor until a rich, thick paste forms. Though it is wonderful here as the unassuming star of a lovely, simple cake topped with a salt-laced chocolate glaze, try swapping hazelnut paste in recipes that call for almond paste (such as the amaretti cookies on page 79 or the almond cake with roasted strawberries on page 36).

HAZELNUT CAKE

½ cup/100 g sugar

¼ cup plus 1 tbsp/35 g ground hazelnuts

½ tsp baking powder

¼ tsp salt

½ cup/115 g unsalted butter,
at room temperature

½ cup/225 g Hazelnut Paste,
cut into small pieces (recipe follows)

2 large eggs, separated

½ tsp pure vanilla extract

SALTED CHOCOLATE GLAZE

2 oz/55 g semisweet chocolate

¼ cup/60 ml heavy cream

2 tbsp unsalted butter

1 tsp salt

To make the cake: Heat the oven to 350°F/180°C. Line the bottom of a 9-in/23-cm round cake pan with parchment paper and butter the paper and the sides of the pan.

Combine the sugar, ground hazelnuts, baking powder, and salt in a medium bowl. Stir to mix well and set aside. In a large bowl, using an electric mixer, cream the butter on medium speed until fluffy.

On medium-high speed, beat in the hazelnut paste a few pieces at a time, beating well after each addition, until the mixture is smooth. Decrease the speed to medium-low and gradually beat in the sugar mixture. Add the egg yolks and beat until a smooth batter forms. Beat in the vanilla.

Place the egg whites in another large bowl and beat on high speed until soft peaks form. Gently fold the egg whites into the hazelnut mixture in three additions, stirring until no white streaks remain. Spoon the batter into the prepared pan, smoothing the top with a rubber spatula.

Bake until the top of the cake is lightly browned and a tester inserted in the center comes out clean, 25 to 30 minutes. Remove from the oven and cool the cake in the pan on a wire rack for 5 minutes. Run a knife around the edge of the cake and remove the cake from the pan, discarding the parchment paper. Cool completely on the rack.

To make the glaze: In a small bowl set over a saucepan of simmering water, melt the chocolate, heavy cream, and butter and whisk until smooth. Whisk in the salt. Remove from the heat and cool slightly. Pour the glaze evenly over the hazelnut cake. Let sit for about 10 minutes until the glaze is slightly set.

Cut the cake into medium-thick wedges to serve.

HAZELNUT PASTE

Makes about 1¾ cups/370 g

2 cups/225 g roasted and skinned hazelnuts, coarsely chopped

2 egg whites

1 cup/100 g confectioners' sugar

In the bowl of a food processor fitted with a steel blade, finely grind the nuts until mealy. Add the egg whites and confectioners' sugar and process until fully combined and a paste forms.

The paste will keep in the refrigerator, tightly wrapped, for up to 2 weeks.

Almond Cake with Balsamic-Roasted Strawberries

SERVES 10

Delicate and lightly sweet, this cake is infused with the rich, nutty flavor of freshly ground almonds. To serve, pile strawberries, slow-roasted into submission with balsamic vinegar, on top of thick slices of cake, or accompany the cake with sweetened whipped cream—or both.

ALMOND CAKE

¾ cup/170 g unsalted butter,
at room temperature

¾ cup/150 g sugar

3 large eggs

½ cup/120 ml whole milk

1 tsp pure vanilla extract

1 tsp pure almond extract

2⅓ cups/350 g ground almonds

¼ tsp salt

2 tsp baking powder

BALSAMIC-ROASTED STRAWBERRIES

1 lb/455 g strawberries,
washed, hulled, and halved

1 tbsp sugar

3 tbsp good-quality balsamic vinegar

To make the cake: Heat the oven to 350°F/180°C. Line the bottom of a 10-in/25-cm springform pan with parchment paper and butter the paper and the sides of the pan.

In a medium bowl, using an electric mixer, cream the butter and sugar on medium-high speed until fluffy. Add the eggs, one at a time, beating well after each addition. Add the milk, vanilla, and almond extract; blend until well incorporated.

In a separate bowl, whisk together the ground almonds, salt, and baking powder. Fold the dry ingredients into the wet mixture and beat until well blended.

Pour the batter into the prepared pan and bake until lightly browned and a tester inserted in the center comes out clean, 30 to 40 minutes. Remove from the oven and cool completely in the pan on a rack, then gently remove the sides of the pan and turn the cake out onto a serving plate.

To roast the strawberries: Decrease the oven temperature to 300°F/ 150°C. Line a baking sheet with parchment paper.

In a medium bowl, toss the halved strawberries with the sugar and balsamic vinegar. Pour the strawberries and sauce onto the prepared baking sheet and spread the berries out evenly (they should lay flat).

Roast until the strawberries are slightly withered but still a bit juicy, about 30 minutes, turning the strawberries with a spatula halfway through the cooking time. Watch so the strawberries do not dry out. Remove from the oven and pour into a bowl to cool completely.

Serve slices of cake topped with the roasted strawberries.

Opera Cake

SERVES 8

The process of constructing an opera cake, a French confection consisting of an almond sponge soaked in coffee syrup, layered with coffee buttercream, and topped with chocolate, is not for the faint of heart. Making each component from scratch is a little time consuming, if not overly difficult. Yet the resulting cake is stunning and sure to be a memorable grand finale to any dinner party. In short, it's worth the extra steps. Save it for special occasions or when you want a weekend baking project. Note that the cake portion is a bit thicker than a traditional opera cake; it makes for easier baking when the batter has more volume.

ALMOND SPONGE CAKE

4 whole large eggs,
at room temperature,
plus 4 egg whites

2 cups/200 g ground almonds

1 cup/200 g confectioners' sugar, sifted

6 tbsp cornstarch

¼ tsp cream of tartar

¼ tsp salt

2 tbsp granulated sugar

4 tbsp unsalted butter,
melted and cooled

COFFEE SYRUP

1 tsp instant espresso powder

1 tbsp water plus ½ cup/120 ml

½ cup/100 g confectioners' sugar

¼ cup/60 ml brandy

continued

COFFEE BUTTERCREAM

2 tsp instant espresso powder

1 tbsp warm whole milk

½ cup/115 g unsalted butter,
at room temperature

2 cups/200 g confectioners' sugar

CHOCOLATE GLAZE

6 tbsp/85 g unsalted butter

7 oz/200 g fine-quality bittersweet chocolate,
coarsely chopped

To make the cake: Heat the oven to 425°F/220°C. Line a 15-by-10-in/ 38-by-25-cm rimmed baking pan with parchment paper, leaving a 1-in/2.5-cm overhang on the short sides.

In a large bowl, using an electric mixer, beat the whole eggs at high speed until they have tripled in volume and form a ribbon in the bowl when the beaters are lifted, 2 to 3 minutes. Decrease the speed to low, add the ground almonds and confectioners' sugar, and mix until just combined. Sift the cornstarch over the batter and gently fold in.

In another large bowl, using an electric mixer with clean, dry beaters, beat the egg whites on medium speed until foamy. Add the cream of tartar and salt and beat until the whites just hold soft peaks. Add the granulated sugar, then increase the speed to high and beat until the whites hold stiff peaks.

Fold one-third of the whites into the almond mixture to lighten, then fold in the remaining whites gently but thoroughly. Fold in the melted butter, then pour the batter into the prepared pan, spreading it gently and evenly with a rubber spatula and being careful not to deflate it (the batter will be about ¼ in/6 mm thick).

Bake until very pale golden and springy to the touch, 8 to 10 minutes. Remove from the oven and cool in the pan on a rack for 10 minutes.

Loosen the edges of the cake with a spatula, then transfer the cake (on the parchment paper) to a cutting board. Cut the cake into three equal pieces along its long sides, carefully peel the paper from the cake, and place the cake pieces on a clean piece of parchment paper.

To make the syrup: Dissolve the espresso powder in the 1 tbsp water; set aside.

Place the confectioners' sugar and remaining ½ cup/120 ml water in a pan and stir until dissolved. Bring the mixture to a boil, decrease the heat, and simmer the syrup, without stirring, for 5 minutes. Remove from the heat and stir in the brandy and espresso. Let cool.

To make the buttercream: Dissolve the espresso powder in the warm milk. In a large bowl, using an electric mixer, cream the butter on medium speed until fluffy, then pour in the espresso and keep mixing until it is well blended. Add the confectioners' sugar, 1 cup/100 g at a time, and beat well to incorporate.

To make the glaze: Melt the butter and all but 2 oz/55 g of the chopped chocolate in a metal bowl set over a saucepan of barely simmering water, stirring occasionally, until smooth. Remove the bowl from the pan and stir in the remaining 2 oz/55 g of chocolate until very smooth. Cool the glaze until it is room temperature, but still fluid.

When ready to assemble, place one section of cake on a plate and, using a pastry brush, soak it with one-third of the coffee syrup, then spread one-third of the buttercream evenly over it. Place the next section of cake on top, soak with coffee syrup, and spread with another third of the buttercream. Place the last cake section on top, soak with the remaining syrup, and spread with the rest of the buttercream, taking care to smooth the surface. Chill in the fridge until the buttercream is set and firm to the touch, then top with the chocolate glaze. Refrigerate until the cake is set. (The cake may be made up to 2 days in advance and stored, lightly covered, in the fridge.)

Let the cake sit at room temperature for at least 10 minutes before cutting into 1-in-/2.5-cm-wide slices to serve.

Banana Cake with Lemon Cream Cheese Frosting and Caramelized Bananas

SERVES 10

For a simpler but still very tasty cake, leave off the frosting and sprinkle the top with a little confectioners' sugar just before serving. The batter may also be baked in a loaf pan (with no frosting) to create a more traditional banana bread. Try adding a handful of chopped walnuts or ½ cup/80 g semisweet chocolate chips if baking as a bread.

BANANA CAKE

2 large eggs

½ tsp pure vanilla extract

½ cup/100 g packed light or dark brown sugar

½ cup/120 ml oil of choice,
such as coconut, olive, vegetable, or canola

2 very ripe bananas, mashed

1 cup/120 g ground almonds

½ cup/55 g cornstarch

1¼ tsp baking powder

½ tsp salt

½ tsp ground cinnamon

½ tsp ground ginger

LEMON CREAM CHEESE FROSTING

8 oz/225 g cream cheese,
at room temperature

1½ cups/150 g confectioners' sugar

Grated zest of 1 organic lemon

1 tbsp fresh lemon juice

continued

CARAMELIZED BANANAS

½ tbsp unsalted butter

3 tbsp packed dark brown sugar

2 small-medium,
firm-ripe bananas, peeled and sliced
into ½-in/12-mm rounds
or sliced lengthwise

¼ cup/60 ml dark rum or fresh orange juice

To make the cake: Heat the oven to 350°F/180°C. Line the bottom of a 9-in/23-cm round cake pan with parchment paper and lightly grease the pan and paper with vegetable oil.

In a large bowl, whisk together the eggs, vanilla, brown sugar, and oil until well combined. Add the mashed bananas and stir well.

In another bowl, whisk together the ground almonds, cornstarch, baking powder, salt, cinnamon, and ginger.

Fold the wet ingredients into the dry ingredients and stir well to combine. Pour the batter into the prepared pan and bake the cake until the surface is lightly browned and a tester inserted into the middle comes out clean, 40 to 50 minutes. Remove from the oven and cool for 10 minutes on a wire rack in the pan before turning it out onto the rack to cool completely.

Meanwhile, to make the frosting: In a large bowl, using an electric mixer, beat the cream cheese on medium speed until softened. Slowly add the confectioners' sugar, lemon zest, and lemon juice and beat until creamy, about 3 minutes. Set aside.

To make the bananas: Melt the butter in a nonstick skillet over medium-high heat. Add the brown sugar and spread the banana slices on top. Cook, undisturbed, for about 20 seconds, then add the rum. Cook for another 10 seconds, then carefully flip the bananas and cook for 45 to 60 seconds more, basting with the pan sauce. Set aside.

When ready to assemble, spread the lemon frosting evenly on top of the cake and top with the caramelized bananas.

Cut the cake into thick wedges to serve. The cake may be made 1 day in advance and stored in the fridge. Serve chilled or at room temperature.

Strawberry-Rhubarb Maple Cake

SERVES 8

The pairing of strawberry and rhubarb is a seasonal classic for good reason. Make this dessert in late spring and summer when rhubarb reaches its zenith. Later in the season, other fruits may be used instead— try 1 lb/450 g of pitted, sliced plums or 1 pt/340 g of blackberries or other favorite berries with good results. Lots of whipped cream to finish is a must.

2 stalks rhubarb, coarsely chopped

1 cup/140 g strawberries, cored and quartered

½ cup/120 ml honey

1 cup/140 g cornmeal

1 tsp baking powder

¼ tsp salt

½ tsp ground cinnamon

2 large eggs

½ cup/120 ml maple syrup

1 tsp pure vanilla extract

¼ cup/60 ml vegetable oil

2 tbsp plain low-fat yogurt

2 tbsp coarse sugar, such as turbinado

Whipped cream for serving

Sliced almonds for serving (optional)

Put the rhubarb and strawberries in a bowl and drizzle with the honey. Let sit at room temperature for an hour or so.

Heat the oven to 350°F/180°C. Line the bottom of a 9-in/23-cm cake pan or a 9-in/23-cm ceramic tart pan with parchment paper and lightly grease the paper and sides of the pan with vegetable oil.

continued

In a large bowl, stir together the cornmeal, baking powder, salt, and ground cinnamon.

In another bowl, whisk the eggs and add the maple syrup, vanilla, vegetable oil, and yogurt. Pour the wet mixture into the dry ingredients and stir until just combined.

Stir in the rhubarb-strawberry mixture, scraping in the fruit juice and honey, and stir to evenly distribute.

Pour the batter into the prepared pan, sprinkle with the coarse sugar, and bake until the cake is slightly golden and springs back when lightly pressed, 30 to 35 minutes. Remove from the oven and cool in the pan on a rack for 10 minutes, then turn out onto the rack to cool completely.

Serve the cake at room temperature or slightly warmed, with generous spoonfuls of whipped cream and sliced almonds (if using) scattered on top.

Apple Tea Cake with Maple Glaze

SERVES 10

This rustic cake is ever so slightly gritty from the cornmeal, and that's a good thing. Lush with butter and maple syrup, it is especially good served with vanilla ice cream or whipped cream. If your apples are very sweet you can use a little less sugar, and if cardamom is not to your liking, try substituting an equivalent amount of ground cinnamon.

APPLE TEA CAKE

¾ cup/150 g sugar

1 cup/140 g cornmeal

1 tsp baking powder

5 tbsp/70 g cold unsalted butter, cut into a few pieces

1 tsp pure vanilla extract

1 large egg, lightly beaten

3 large Granny Smith apples, peeled, cored, and very thinly sliced

MAPLE GLAZE

3 tbsp maple syrup

3 tbsp unsalted butter, melted and cooled slightly

2 tsp ground cardamom

To make the cake: Heat the oven to 350°F/180°C. Butter a 9-in/ 23-cm springform pan.

In the bowl of a food processor fitted with a steel blade, combine the sugar, cornmeal, and baking powder. Pulse to mix coarsely. Add the butter and pulse until no large lumps remain. Add the vanilla and egg and pulse to blend well. Pour the batter into the prepared pan and spread it evenly with a rubber spatula. Arrange the apple slices over the batter in a circular pattern and place in the oven to bake.

continued

Meanwhile, to make the glaze: Combine the maple syrup, melted butter, and ground cardamom in a small bowl and whisk to blend well.

After the cake has baked for about 45 minutes, remove from the oven and spoon the glaze evenly over it. Bake until the apple slices are slightly caramelized and a tester inserted into the middle of the cake comes out clean, another 20 minutes or so.

Remove the cake from the oven and place the pan on a wire rack; cool for 20 minutes. Run a knife around the edge of the pan to release the cake and remove the sides.

Cool completely before serving. The cake may be stored, wrapped in aluminum foil or in an airtight container, for up to 5 days.

Plum Cakes

MAKES 12 CAKES

Use plums that are not overly ripe; for best results they should be
on the firmer side so that they will hold their integrity when baked
and not turn into mush. For a chocolate version, substitute ⅓ cup/35 g
of unsweetened cocoa powder for the cornstarch.

½ cup/60 g shelled pistachios
½ cup/60 g skinned hazelnuts
½ cup/100 g packed light or dark brown sugar
⅓ cup/40 g cornstarch
¼ tsp ground cinnamon
¼ tsp salt
2 large eggs
½ cup/120 ml coconut milk
4 tbsp/40 ml olive oil
4 plums, pitted and thinly sliced
¼ cup/50 g raw sugar

Heat the oven to 350°F/180°C. Line a 12-cup cupcake tin with cupcake
liners.

In the bowl of a food processor fitted with a steel blade, finely grind
the pistachios and hazelnuts. Place the ground nuts in a large bowl and
whisk in the brown sugar, cornstarch, cinnamon, and salt.

In another bowl, whisk the eggs with the coconut milk until well
blended. Stir in the olive oil and add the egg mixture to the dry ingredients. Stir with a spoon and then whisk until the batter is smooth.

Divide the batter between the wells of the cupcake tins. Arrange 3 or
4 plum slices and sprinkle the raw sugar on top of each cake.

Bake until the tops of the cakes are golden and a tester inserted into the
middle of a cake comes out clean, about 30 minutes. Remove from the
oven and cool in the tin on a wire rack for 10 minutes, then turn out onto
the rack to cool completely. The cakes will firm as they cool. Chill the
cakes for at least 2 hours before serving to solidify the crumb.

Polenta Cake

SERVES 10

This cake is simple to make and produces an utterly lovely result. Light and fluffy from the butter, not too sweet, and with a hint of lemon, it's the perfect finish to a winter lunch party—with a generous helping of whipped cream and a spoonful of fruit compote—or plain with a cup of tea anytime.

1 cup/140 g polenta

⅔ cup/50 g ground almonds

1½ tsp baking powder

½ tsp salt

½ cup/50 g unsalted butter, at room temperature

2 tbsp finely grated lemon zest, plus 2 tbsp fresh lemon juice, from an organic lemon

1 cup/200 g granulated sugar

2 large eggs

½ cup/120 ml sour cream

1 tsp pure vanilla extract

3 tbsp coarse sugar, such as turbinado

Fruit compote for serving (optional)

Whipped cream for serving (optional)

Heat the oven to 350°F/180°C. Butter a 9-in/23-cm cake pan. Dust the pan with polenta, tapping out any excess.

Sift the polenta, ground almonds, baking powder, and salt into a medium bowl. Using an electric mixer, beat the butter in large bowl until smooth and fluffy. Beat in the lemon zest. Gradually add the granulated sugar and beat on medium-high speed until light and fluffy, occasionally scraping down the sides of the bowl. Add the eggs, one at a time, beating well after each addition. Beat in the sour cream, lemon juice, and vanilla. Fold in the dry ingredients in three additions until just incorporated.

Pour the batter into the prepared pan and smooth the top with a rubber spatula. Sprinkle with the coarse sugar.

Bake the cake until a tester inserted into the center comes out clean, 25 to 30 minutes. Cool in the pan on a wire rack for 10 minutes, then run a knife around the pan sides to loosen. Turn the cake out onto a plate, then invert onto the rack, sugar-side up, and cool completely.

Cut the cake into slices and top with fruit compote and whipped cream, if desired (it's just as delicious unadorned), to serve.

Lime Cornmeal Cake with Lime Curd

SERVES 10

The delicate flavor of lime marks this layer cake made from cornmeal and ground almonds. Let the cake rest in the refrigerator for a few hours to allow the flavors to really mingle, then bring it to room temperature for about a half hour before serving.

LIME CORNMEAL CAKE

1 cup/225 g unsalted butter,
at room temperature

1 cup plus 2 tbsp/225 g sugar

1½ cups/180 g ground almonds

1 tsp pure vanilla extract

3 large eggs, lightly beaten

Grated zest of 2 organic limes, plus
fresh juice of 1 lime

1 cup/140 g cornmeal

1 tsp baking powder

⅛ tsp salt

LIME CURD

3 large eggs

¾ cup/150 g sugar

⅓ cup/75 ml fresh lime juice, plus
grated zest of 1 organic lime

4 tbsp/55 g unsalted butter,
cut into small pieces

Crème fraîche or
whipped cream for serving

To make the cake: Heat the oven to 325°F/165°C. Lightly butter a 9-in/23-cm springform pan and line the bottom with parchment paper.

In a large bowl, using an electric mixer, beat the butter on medium speed until creamy, about 3 minutes. Add the sugar and beat until light and fluffy, about 2 minutes. Stir in the ground almonds and vanilla. Whisk in the eggs, a little bit at a time, whisking well to incorporate.

Fold in the lime zest, lime juice, cornmeal, baking powder, and salt. Stir well to combine. Pour the batter into the prepared pan and bake until the cake is deep golden in color and a tester inserted into the middle comes out clean, about 50 minutes. Remove from the oven and cool in the pan on a wire rack for 10 minutes. Turn out of the pan onto the rack and cool completely.

Meanwhile, to make the curd: In a metal bowl placed over a saucepan of simmering water, whisk together the eggs, sugar, and lime juice until blended.

Cook, stirring constantly to prevent curdling, until the mixture becomes thick, about 10 minutes. Remove from the heat and immediately pour through a fine-mesh strainer into a bowl to remove any lumps. Add the butter pieces to the mixture and whisk until the butter has melted. Stir in the lime zest and let cool.

With a serrated knife, halve the cooled cake horizontally. Spread the bottom layer with about ½ cup/115 g of the lime curd. Top with the second cake layer and spread with another ½ cup/115 g curd. (You may have leftover lime curd, which is wonderful spread on toast or muffins or folded into plain yogurt.)

Serve slices of the cake with dollops of crème fraîche or whipped cream.

Lemon Loaf

SERVES 8

This loaf cake is reminiscent of a traditional pound cake, but almond paste
stands in for the flour and lemon zest gives it a bit of a citrusy zing.
It is delicious spread with softened cream cheese or butter. Almond paste
is very easy to make from scratch, but it's just as easy to purchase
at the grocery store instead.

½ cup/125 g Almond Paste
(recipe follows)

¼ cup/50 g sugar

½ cup/115 g unsalted butter,
at room temperature

3 large eggs

½ cup/55 g cornstarch

1 tsp baking powder

¼ tsp salt

Grated zest of 1 organic lemon

Heat the oven to 325°F/165°C. Line a 9-by-5-in/23-by-13-cm loaf pan
with parchment paper.

Place the almond paste and sugar in the bowl of a food processor fitted
with a steel blade and process until it is a crumbly texture. Add the
butter and eggs and process until fully incorporated. Stop the processor
and scrape down the sides and bottom of the bowl with a rubber spatula.

In a small bowl, whisk together the cornstarch, baking powder, salt,
and lemon zest, then add the mixture to the food processor. Pulse until
combined; you want a smooth batter. Pour the batter into the prepared
pan and bake until a tester inserted in the middle comes out clean,
45 to 50 minutes.

Remove the cake from the pan and cool on a wire rack to room temperature.

Cut generous slices from the loaf to serve. The loaf may be stored, tightly wrapped in plastic wrap, at room temperature for up to 5 days.

ALMOND PASTE

Makes 1½ cups/370 g

1½ cups/225 g whole raw almonds

1½ cups/150 g confectioners' sugar, sifted

1 egg white, lightly beaten,
at room temperature

½ tsp pure almond extract

Place the almonds and ½ cup/50 g of the confectioners' sugar in the bowl of a food processor fitted with a steel blade. Process the nuts and sugar until the nuts are very finely ground, stopping periodically to scrape down the sides of the bowl with a rubber spatula.

Once the almonds are very finely ground, add the rest of the confectioners' sugar and pulse until it is completely mixed into the ground almonds.

Stop the processor and add the egg white and almond extract. Process the almond paste until it comes together in a clump. (If it seems very sticky, add a little more confectioners' sugar, a spoonful at a time, until it is smooth.)

The paste will keep, tightly wrapped, in the fridge for up to 2 weeks.

Walnut Torte with Coffee Cream

SERVES 10

Tortes are classic, nut-based European desserts that also happen to be naturally flourless. More elaborate tortes call for slicing the cake into layers and filling with a rich, fudgy frosting. This version of a walnut torte is a bit simpler but no less appealing, with the inclusion of coffee-infused whipped cream perfectly complementing the deep nutty flavor of the walnuts. Serve with cups of espresso or strong tea.

WALNUT TORTE

1¾ cups/135 g raw walnuts

4 large eggs, separated

½ cup/100 g granulated sugar

COFFEE CREAM

1 cup/240 ml heavy whipping cream, chilled

3 tbsp confectioners' sugar

1 tsp instant coffee crystals dissolved in 2 tsp heavy whipping cream

½ tsp vanilla extract

To make the torte: Heat the oven to 350°F/180°C. Butter the bottom of a 9-in/23-cm springform pan.

Spread the walnuts on a baking sheet, place in the oven, and toast until lightly browned and nutty-smelling, about 10 minutes. Remove from the oven and set aside to cool completely.

Place the walnuts in the bowl of a food processor fitted with a steel blade and process until finely ground. In a large bowl, beat the egg yolks with an electric mixer on medium speed until light and fluffy, about 4 minutes. Gradually add the granulated sugar, beating until well blended. Stir the ground walnuts into the yolk mixture.

In another large bowl, using an electric mixer with clean, dry beaters, beat the egg whites until stiff but not dry. Fold the whites gently into the nut mixture in two additions. Pour the batter into the prepared pan.

Bake the cake until a tester inserted into the center comes out clean, about 40 minutes. Cool for 5 minutes in the pan, then run a knife between the cake and the pan sides to loosen, and remove the pan sides. Cool the cake completely on a wire rack (the cake will fall in the center).

To make the coffee cream: When you are ready to serve the cake, in a large bowl, using an electric mixer, beat the cream, confectioners' sugar, coffee mixture, and vanilla on medium-high speed until stiff peaks form.

Spread the coffee cream on top of the cake just before serving. The cake may be made 1 day in advance and stored, tightly wrapped, in the fridge. Wait until serving to spread it with the coffee cream.

Cherry Clafoutis

SERVES 8

A clafoutis is a French dessert traditionally made with unpitted black cherries, though I prefer to remove the pits before baking for ease of consumption and use the more commonly found red cherries. Other fruits such as blackberries, sliced plums, or apples may be incorporated instead in an equivalent amount to the cherries (the dessert would then be termed a *flaugnarde*).

4 large eggs, separated

⅔ cup/130 g sugar

3 tbsp cornstarch

3 tbsp cornmeal

2 tsp pure vanilla extract

1 cup/240 ml heavy cream

½ tsp salt

1½ lb/680 g fresh cherries
(or frozen cherries, thawed and drained),
pitted

1 tsp grated zest
from 1 organic lemon

Vanilla ice cream for serving

Heat the oven to 375°F/190°C. Butter a 9-in/23-cm ceramic tart pan or a baking dish that is either 9 by 9 in/23 by 23 cm or 10 by 7 in/25 by 17 cm.

In a large bowl, combine the egg yolks and ⅓ cup/65 g of the sugar. Using an electric mixer, beat the egg mixture on medium-high speed until a ribbon of the egg-sugar mixture forms in the bowl when the beaters are lifted, about 8 minutes. Add the cornstarch, cornmeal, vanilla, and cream. Decrease the speed to low and beat until completely blended, 3 to 4 minutes, stopping the mixer occasionally to scrape down the sides of the bowl.

In a small bowl, whisk the egg whites and salt for about 30 seconds. Add the whisked whites to the batter and beat with the mixer on low speed until incorporated, 1 to 2 minutes.

Preheat the prepared baking dish in the oven for about 4 minutes.

In a bowl, stir together the cherries, the remaining 1/3 cup/65 g sugar, and the lemon zest. Remove the pan from the oven (it will be hot!), pour in the cherries, and top with the batter. Bake until the clafoutis is set in the middle, 30 to 35 minutes.

Remove from the oven and immediately portion into dessert bowls. Top with vanilla ice cream to serve.

Pavlova with Cream and Berries

SERVES 8

A pavlova—a meringue-like dessert believed to have originated in either Australia or New Zealand and named after Russian ballerina Anna Pavlova—is typically served with berries and whipped cream. The recipe can also be doubled, baked into layers, and served as a layer cake of sorts. Here, things are kept simple: whipped cream is spread into the softly sunken center of the pavlova and lots of fresh fruit is piled on top. For a lighter dessert, leave out the whipped cream and use the light topping variation (recipe follows).

1 cup/200 g sugar

1 tbsp cornstarch

4 egg whites, at room temperature

¼ tsp salt

3 tbsp cold water

1 tsp distilled white vinegar

1 cup/240 ml heavy cream

4 cups/455 g mixed berries
or sliced fruit of choice

Lightly toasted sliced almonds
for garnish (optional)

Heat the oven to 300°F/150°C. Trace a circle that is approximately 8 in/20 cm on a sheet of parchment paper. Turn the parchment over and set the paper on a baking sheet.

In a small bowl, whisk together the sugar and cornstarch.

In a large bowl, using an electric mixer, beat the egg whites with the salt on medium speed until they hold soft peaks. Add the cold water (the whites will loosen) and beat until the whites again hold soft peaks.

continued

Increase the speed to medium-high and beat in the sugar mixture, 1 tbsp at a time. After all of the sugar mixture has been added, beat for 1 minute more.

Add the vinegar and beat on high speed until the meringue is glossy and holds stiff peaks, about 5 minutes.

Gently spread the meringue inside the circle on the parchment paper, making the edge of the meringue slightly higher than its center. Bake until the meringue is pale golden and has a crust, about 45 minutes (the inside will still be marshmallow-like).

Turn off the oven and slightly prop open the oven door with a wooden spoon. Cool the meringue in the oven for 1 hour.

When ready to assemble, place the cooled meringue on a large plate. Beat the heavy cream until it just holds stiff peaks. Spread the whipped cream evenly over the top of the pavlova and top with berries before serving.

LIGHT TOPPING VARIATION

2 cups/225 g blueberries
or blackberries

1 tbsp maple syrup

Grated zest and fresh juice
of 1 small organic lime

Place the blueberries, maple syrup, lime zest, and lime juice in a small bowl and let marinate for at least 20 minutes at room temperature before using.

Strawberry Soufflé

SERVES 6

I was inspired by my farmers' market to make this enticingly light and delicate soufflé. When strawberries are in season, they're hard to resist. Then I started thinking about other berries that might work, too: blackberries, blueberries, raspberries. You want about 1 cup/240 ml of puréed fruit per recipe, so adjust the type of berry according to your taste (a combination might be wonderful, too).

About 20 strawberries, cored and halved

6 tbsp/65 g sugar

1 tbsp cornstarch

**1 tsp grated zest
from 1 organic lemon**

⅛ tsp pure vanilla extract

4 egg whites

Heat the oven to 400°F/200°C. Lightly grease a 2-qt/2-L soufflé dish or six individual ½-cup/120-ml ramekins with vegetable oil.

In a the bowl of a food processor fitted with a steel blade or in a blender, coarsely purée the strawberries, 3 tbsp of the sugar, and the cornstarch, then transfer to a small saucepan. Stir over medium heat until the mixture boils and thickens, about 3 minutes. Whisk in the lemon zest and vanilla. Remove from the heat and cool completely.

In a large bowl, using an electric mixer, beat the egg whites on high speed until soft peaks form. Add the remaining 3 tbsp sugar and beat until stiff but not dry. Fold the strawberry purée gently into the beaten whites in three additions, stirring until just incorporated and no white streaks remain.

Transfer to the prepared dish or ramekins. Bake until the soufflé is puffed and golden, about 25 minutes for the soufflé dish and 15 minutes for the ramekins.

Serve immediately.

Chocolate Soufflé Cupcakes with Salted Caramel Buttercream

MAKES 12 CUPCAKES

Salted caramel sauce is a guilty pleasure of mine: Is it more sweet? Or more salty? In the end it doesn't much matter, it's simply "good." And when folded into a creamy buttercream frosting that is then perched atop fudgy chocolate cupcakes, it becomes absolutely addicting. Though it may seem difficult to eat just one cupcake, these are so rich you'll probably be satiated (after licking up the crumbs, of course) for at least a few hours.

CHOCOLATE SOUFFLÉ CUPCAKES

6 oz/170 g bittersweet or semisweet chocolate, chopped

6 tbsp/85 g unsalted butter, cut into pieces

3 large eggs, separated

6 tbsp/50 g granulated sugar

¼ tsp salt

1 tsp pure vanilla extract

SALTED CARAMEL BUTTERCREAM

½ cup/80 g unsalted butter, at room temperature

2 to 3 cups/200 to 300 g confectioners' sugar

¼ cup/60 ml Salted Caramel Sauce (page 20)

1 to 2 tbsp whole milk

To make the cupcakes: Heat the oven to 350°F/180°C. Line a 12-cup cupcake tin with cupcake liners.

Put the chocolate and butter in a heavy saucepan and cook over low heat, stirring, until fully melted and smooth. Remove from the heat and cool to lukewarm.

In a medium bowl, using an electric mixer, beat the egg yolks and sugar on medium-high speed until the mixture is very thick and pale, about 2 minutes. Beat in the chocolate mixture, salt, and vanilla. In a large bowl, beat the egg whites on high speed with an electric mixer until medium-firm peaks form. Gently fold the egg whites into the chocolate mixture in three additions, folding until no white streaks remain.

Divide the batter among the prepared cups, filling each about three-quarters of the way. Bake the cupcakes until the tops are puffed and dry to the touch and a tester inserted into the centers comes out mostly clean, with some moist crumbs attached, 15 to 20 minutes.

Remove the cupcakes from the oven and let sit in the tin for 5 minutes before turning out onto a wire rack to cool completely.

To make the buttercream: In a large bowl, using an electric mixer, cream the butter on medium-high speed. Beat in the confectioners' sugar 1 cup/100 g at a time, beating well until smooth. Add the caramel sauce, beating until it is fully incorporated and glossy.

When ready to frost, spread each cupcake with a generous amount of buttercream.

Store at room temperature in an airtight container, or in the fridge, for up to 5 days.

Peanut Butter–Chocolate Cupcakes with Dark Chocolate Frosting

MAKES 12 CUPCAKES

I love the flavor combination of peanut butter and chocolate and am always looking for an excuse to incorporate it into my daily life. This naturally flourless cupcake recipe is dense and not overly sweet, making it the perfect vehicle for lots of creamy dark chocolate frosting.

PEANUT BUTTER–CHOCOLATE CUPCAKES

1¼ cups/280 g natural peanut butter

1 cup/200 g packed light or dark brown sugar

½ cup/120 ml whole milk

4 large eggs, separated

½ tsp pure vanilla extract

1 tsp baking soda

¾ tsp baking powder

½ tsp salt

DARK CHOCOLATE FROSTING

½ cup/115 g unsalted butter, at room temperature

4 oz/115 g semisweet chocolate, melted

1 cup/100 g confectioners' sugar

To make the cupcakes: Heat the oven to 350°F/180°C. Line a 12-cup cupcake tin with cupcake liners.

In a large bowl, stir together the peanut butter, brown sugar, milk, egg yolks, vanilla, baking soda, baking powder, and salt until combined. Alternatively, use an electric mixer on medium speed to combine the ingredients until smooth. In a second large bowl, beat the egg whites with an electric mixer on high speed until stiff peaks form. Gently fold the egg whites into the peanut butter mixture and stir until completely incorporated.

Divide the batter among the prepared cups. Bake the cupcakes until the tops are puffed and dry to the touch and a tester inserted into the centers comes out mostly clean, with some moist crumbs attached, 15 to 20 minutes.

Remove the cupcakes from the oven and let sit in the tin for 5 minutes before turning out onto a wire rack to cool completely.

To make the frosting: In a large bowl, using an electric mixer, cream the butter on high speed until fluffy, then add the melted chocolate. Beat well to combine. Add the confectioners' sugar, a little at a time, until well blended.

When ready to frost, spread each cupcake with a generous amount of frosting, swirling decoratively with the back of a spoon if you like.

Store at room temperature in an airtight container, or in the fridge, for up to 5 days.

Carrot Cake Cupcakes with Maple Cream Cheese Frosting

MAKES 12 CUPCAKES

These coconut-flecked, vividly orange cakes caused a friend's two-year-old to wake up one morning asking for another helping. I take that as a ringing endorsement. Topped by a cream cheese frosting generously sweetened with maple syrup, it's clear why he liked them so much. Be sure to let the cupcakes cool completely before icing and try to allow for at least 30 minutes chilling in the fridge to help solidify the crumb.

CARROT CAKE CUPCAKES

7 tbsp/100 g unsalted butter, at room temperature

3 large eggs

1 cup/60 g unsweetened flaked coconut

3 large carrots, grated

2/3 cup/130 g sugar

1/2 cup/55 g cornstarch

1 tsp pure vanilla extract

1 1/2 tsp baking powder

1/2 tsp salt

1/2 cup/85 g raisins

1/2 cup/60 g chopped walnuts

MAPLE CREAM CHEESE FROSTING

8 oz/225 g cream cheese, at room temperature

2 tbsp unsalted butter, at room temperature

3 tbsp maple syrup

To make the cupcakes: Heat the oven to 350°F/180°C. Line a 12-cup cupcake tin with cupcake liners.

Put the butter, eggs, coconut, three-quarters of the grated carrots, the sugar, cornstarch, vanilla, baking powder, and salt in the bowl of a food processor fitted with a steel blade and process until a smooth batter forms, at least 1 minute. Stir in the remaining carrots, the raisins, and walnuts.

Divide the batter among the prepared cups. Bake the cupcakes until the tops are lightly browned, firm to the touch, and a tester inserted into the centers comes out clean, about 20 minutes.

Remove the cupcakes from the oven and let sit in the tin for 5 minutes before turning out onto a wire rack to cool completely.

To make the frosting: In a large bowl, using an electric mixer, combine the cream cheese, butter, and maple syrup and beat on medium speed until very well combined and smooth.

When ready to frost, spread each cupcake with an equal amount of frosting and refrigerate for at least 30 minutes before serving.

Store at room temperature in an airtight container, or in the fridge, for up to 5 days.

Vanilla Cupcakes with Lemon Buttercream

MAKES 12 CUPCAKES

A riff on an angel food cake, these cupcakes come together quickly. Finished with a cap of bright, lemony buttercream, they usher in spring in a burst of fresh flavor. You can save and freeze unused egg whites until you have enough to make this recipe. (Egg whites will keep safely in the freezer for up to 12 months; thaw them overnight in the fridge and bring to room temperature just before using.) Grate a little extra zest for garnish, if you like.

VANILLA CUPCAKES

½ cup plus 2 tbsp/55 g cornstarch

½ cup/100 g granulated sugar

6 egg whites

¾ tsp cream of tartar

1 tsp pure vanilla extract

⅛ tsp salt

LEMON BUTTERCREAM

½ cup/115 g unsalted butter, at room temperature

2 tbsp grated lemon zest, plus 1 tbsp fresh lemon juice from 1 organic lemon

1 cup/100 g confectioners' sugar

1 to 2 tbsp whole milk, if needed

continued

To make the cupcakes: Heat the oven to 350°F/180°C. Line a 12-cup cupcake tin with cupcake liners.

In a medium bowl, sift together the cornstarch and granulated sugar and set aside. In a large bowl, beat the egg whites with an electric mixer on high speed until frothy, about 1 minute. Add the cream of tartar, vanilla, and salt and beat until stiff peaks form, 5 to 6 minutes. Sprinkle one-quarter of the cornstarch mixture over the egg whites and fold in gently. Repeat until all the cornstarch mixture is incorporated.

Divide the batter among the prepared cups. Bake the cupcakes until the tops are lightly golden and springy to the touch, 10 to 15 minutes.

Remove the cupcakes from the oven and cool completely in the tin on a wire rack.

To make the buttercream: In a large bowl, using an electric mixer, cream the butter on medium speed until fluffy. Add the lemon zest, lemon juice, and confectioners' sugar and beat well to combine. Add a little milk if the buttercream is too dry. Whip on high speed until it is fluffy and thick, 3 to 5 minutes.

When ready to frost, spread each cupcake with a generous amount of buttercream.

Store in an airtight container or in the fridge for up to 5 days.

Cookies and Other Treats

One of my early flourless baking attempts fell flat—literally. I'd baked a batch of tiny chocolate cakes in a mini muffin tin for a holiday party and no matter how long I let the batter sit in the oven, the damned things did not rise. When I pried them from the tin they flopped, certainly not the pretty little cupcakes I'd envisioned. When I tasted one just to see (and because I hate to waste good ingredients), I was happily surprised to find they weren't half bad. Actually, they were quite good. I served them to my guests, passing them off as "fudge cookies," and none were the wiser. I preferred those "cakes" as cookies anyway.

As I embarked upon testing cookie recipes for this cookbook, I fine-tuned that "disaster" to the point that the cake idea was just a distant memory. I also took that lesson to heart: Seeming failures can sometimes become our greatest successes if we just look at them from another angle.

I love every single recipe in this chapter. Some are traditional flourless cookies, such as macaroons (but here with the addition of lemon zest and honey to keep things interesting) and meringues, as well as Italian amaretti (with almond paste and egg whites), and French macarons (nutty sandwich cookies with a variety of fillings).

And there are the less expected, such as halvah-like Sesame-Tahini Cookies—dry, not-too-sweet, and perfect with afternoon coffee; chewy, molasses-infused cinnamon cookies; chocolate spice cookies, fiery with ginger; and delicate, lightly salted lavender-lemon cookies made from ground oats. I have also included a few sweet breads—the Pumpkin Bread makes an especially fine seasonal treat, and any berry that suits your fancy can be incorporated into the Honeyed Blueberry Cakes. You'll also find my very favorite brownie rendition and a version of a peanut butter-and-jelly bar.

I believe that cookies are the backbone of the baker's kitchen, the sometimes homely but always appreciated staples of the dessert reportoire. For a quick flourless fix, or for anytime, cookies are a sure bet.

Amaretti

MAKES ABOUT 20 COOKIES

Delicate and light, amaretti are dry Italian cookies made with almond paste and egg whites. Watch carefully so that the cookies don't burn; they are done when their surfaces just turn golden brown and crack slightly.

7 oz/200 g Almond Paste (page 57),
broken into small pieces
1 cup/200 g sugar
2 egg whites

Position the rack in the center of the oven and heat the oven to 375°F/190°C. Line a baking sheet with parchment paper.

Put the almond paste and sugar in the bowl of a food processor fitted with a steel blade. Pulse until the mixture is very fine. Add the egg whites, one at a time, processing well after each addition. Continue processing the dough until very smooth, about 1 minute. (If using an electric mixer, cut the almond paste into pieces and place in a large, deep bowl. Beat on low speed with the sugar to break up any lumps. Add the egg whites, one at a time, beating well after each addition. Keep beating the dough until it is very smooth, about 3 minutes.)

Scoop out small balls of dough with a teaspoon and drop them onto the prepared baking sheet about 1 in/2.5 cm apart (the dough will be very sticky). Bake until the cookies have risen, are a deep golden color, and have tiny cracks in their surfaces, 12 to 15 minutes (you may need to bake in two batches).

Remove the baking sheet from the oven and place on a wire rack to cool completely. When the cookies are cool, gently peel them from the parchment paper.

Store in an airtight container at room temperature for up to 5 days, but they are best eaten fresh.

DRIED APRICOT VARIATION:

Add ½ cup/110 g chopped dried apricots after beating in the egg whites. Stir until they are well incorporated and proceed as directed.

Macarons

MAKES ABOUT 24 COOKIES

Macarons, French sandwich cookies, are made from ground nuts, egg whites, and confectioners' sugar and filled with a variety of flavors. This recipe calls for almonds, but the beauty of these little gems is that any nuts may be substituted with wonderful results. Try an equivalent amount of ground nuts, such as pistachios or hazelnuts, for the almonds. A pastry bag fitted with a plain tip is called for to form the cookies. Alternatively, you may use a teaspoon to scoop and drop the egg white mixture onto the prepared baking sheets. The cookies will not be as uniformly round, but will taste exactly the same.

2 cups/200 g confectioners' sugar,
sifted

1 cup/100 g sliced almonds,
finely ground

4 egg whites,
at room temperature

¼ cup/50 g granulated sugar

Filling of choice:
chocolate ganache (see page 32),
lemon curd (see page 139),
or fruit jam

Position the racks in the upper and lower third of the oven and heat the oven to 350°F/180°C. Line two baking sheets with parchment paper and have a pastry bag with a plain tip (about ½ in/12 mm) ready.

Put the confectioners' sugar and almonds in the bowl of a food processor fitted with a steel blade and process until well combined and there are no lumps. (Alternatively, sift together three times.)

In a large bowl, using an electric mixer, beat the egg whites on medium-high speed until they begin to hold soft peaks. Add the granulated sugar, 1 tbsp at a time, and continue beating until the egg whites are very stiff and firm, about 2 minutes.

Using a rubber spatula, carefully fold the almond mixture into the beaten egg whites in two batches. When the mixture is smooth and there are no streaks of egg white, stop folding and scrape the batter into a pastry bag.

Pipe the batter on the prepared baking sheets in 1 in/2.5 cm circles (about 1 tbsp of batter each), evenly spaced about 1 in/2.5 cm apart. With a damp fingertip, gently smooth any pointy tips.

Bake until the tops are firm and slightly golden, 10 to 15 minutes. Remove the cookies from the oven and let cool for 5 minutes on the baking sheets, then peel them from the parchment paper and place on a wire rack to cool completely.

When ready to assemble, turn half of the cookies bottom-side up. Spread a thin layer of filling (about 1 tsp) over the cookie bottoms. Press a plain cookie, bottom-side down, onto the filling.

Store in an airtight container at room temperature for up to 3 days.

Coconut-Lemon Macaroons

MAKES 24 COOKIES

I love the bright lemon flavor that sings through these macaroons, which are traditionally made with shredded coconut and egg whites. In this version, honey is swapped for granulated sugar to keep things interesting. Try dipping some of the baked cookies in melted semisweet chocolate or add a handful of fresh blueberries to the batter. Often served as part of a Passover repast, these cookies taste light, fresh, and full of spring.

2 egg whites
Grated zest from 1 organic lemon
¼ cup plus 2 tbsp/130 g honey
½ tsp pure vanilla extract
**2½ cups/180 g shredded,
unsweetened coconut**

Position the rack in the middle of the oven and heat the oven to 300°F/150°C. Line a baking sheet with parchment paper.

In a medium bowl, whisk the egg whites for about 30 seconds to lighten them up a bit. Whisk in the lemon zest, honey, and vanilla. Add the shredded coconut and stir well to combine.

Scoop out 1 tbsp portions of the coconut mixture. Using your hands, squeeze to compress the mixture and roll each into a small ball. Place them on the prepared baking sheet about 1 in/2.5 cm apart.

Bake until the bottoms and edges of the cookies are just starting to brown, 15 to 20 minutes. Remove from the oven and let cool completely on the baking sheet. When fully cooled, peel the cookies from the paper before serving.

Store in an airtight container at room temperature for up to 5 days.

Ginger-Chocolate Snaps

MAKES 24 COOKIES

The sharp bite of ginger is tempered in these cookies by the gentling flavor of chocolate and is balanced by notes of brown sugar and almonds.

¼ cup/60 g unsalted butter, at room temperature

⅔ cup/130 g packed dark brown sugar

1 large egg

½ tsp pure vanilla extract

4 oz/112 g bittersweet chocolate, chopped, melted, and cooled

½ cup/60 g ground almonds

¼ cup/30 g unsweetened cocoa powder

1 tsp baking powder

3 tbsp ground ginger

1 tsp ground cinnamon

½ tsp ground cloves

¼ tsp salt

2 tbsp granulated sugar

Heat the oven to 350°F/180°C. Line two baking sheets with parchment.

In a large bowl, using an electric mixer, beat the butter with the brown sugar on medium-high speed until light and fluffy, about 2 minutes. Beat in the egg and vanilla. Stir in the chocolate.

In another bowl, whisk together the ground almonds, cocoa powder, baking powder, ginger, cinnamon, cloves, and salt. Fold the almond mixture into the butter mixture and mix until well combined. Cover with plastic wrap and refrigerate until the dough is firm enough to roll, about 20 minutes.

Using a small scoop or a teaspoon, scoop out portions of the dough and roll into balls. Place them on the prepared baking sheets about 1 in/2.5 cm apart, flatten gently with a fork, and sprinkle with granulated sugar.

Bake until the cookies are slightly firm, 12 to 15 minutes. Remove from the oven, cool on the baking sheets for 5 minutes, then transfer the cookies to a rack to cool completely.

Store in an airtight container at room temperature for up to 5 days.

Almond Butter–Chocolate Chip Cookies

MAKES 30 COOKIES

Crisply delicious and with a wonderful crunch, these are the cookies that started off my preoccupation with flourless desserts. You can make your own almond (and nut) butter easily by processing raw almonds in a food processor fitted with a steel blade for a few minutes, scraping down the sides of the bowl occasionally, until it forms a well-blended and creamy paste. Almond butter is also readily available at health food stores and some supermarkets.

1 cup/230 g almond butter

½ cup/100 g packed light or dark brown sugar

½ cup/100 g granulated sugar

1 large egg

1 tsp baking soda

2 tbsp maple syrup

1 tsp pure vanilla extract

¼ tsp salt

½ cup/55 g slivered almonds

½ cup/85 g semisweet chocolate chips

Heat the oven to 350°F/180°C. Line two baking sheets with parchment paper.

In a large bowl, stir together the almond butter and both sugars until well combined. Add the egg, baking soda, maple syrup, vanilla, and salt and stir well to combine. Stir in the almonds and chocolate chips.

Scoop out 1-tsp portions of dough and roll into balls. Place them on the prepared baking sheets about 1 in/2.5 cm apart and flatten gently with a fork.

Bake until the cookies are lightly browned, 10 to 12 minutes. Remove from the oven and cool on the baking sheets for 5 minutes before serving.

Store in an airtight container at room temperature for up to 1 week.

Chocolate Chocolate Chip Cookies

MAKES 20 TO 24 COOKIES

These cookies, like many flourless baked goods, rely on egg whites for their lift. They are a bit meringue-like, though not as chewy, and include a smattering of semisweet chocolate chips to give a little crunch. I love sprinkling sea salt across the tops of the cookies just before baking to bring out their deep chocolate flavor.

2½ cups/150 g confectioners' sugar

½ cup/50 g unsweetened cocoa powder

¼ tsp ground cinnamon

1 tsp salt

3 egg whites

1 cup/170 g semisweet chocolate chips

Heat the oven to 350°F/180°C. Line two baking sheets with parchment paper.

In a large bowl, whisk together the confectioners' sugar, cocoa powder, cinnamon, and ¼ tsp of the salt. Using an electric mixer, beat in the egg whites on medium speed until well combined; the mixture should be sticky and glossy. Fold in the chocolate chips.

Scoop out 2-tsp portions of the dough and drop them onto the prepared baking sheets about 2 in/5 cm apart. Sprinkle with the remaining salt. Bake until the surfaces are set and slightly cracked, 13 to 15 minutes. Remove from the oven and cool completely on the baking sheets (use a spatula to remove the cooled cookies).

Store in an airtight container at room temperature for up to 1 week.

Oatmeal–Chocolate Chip Cookies

MAKES 24 COOKIES

Oats whirled with peanut butter seems almost as natural a combination as peanut butter and chocolate, and indeed the addition of chocolate chips here sends these cookies into the realm of the sublime. Though it's difficult not to eat them as soon as they come out of the oven, when cooled completely these cookies make great, sturdy cookies for ice cream sandwiches, particularly with vanilla ice cream.

¼ cup/55 g unsalted butter, at room temperature

1 cup/255 g creamy peanut butter

¾ cup/140 g packed light or dark brown sugar

½ cup/100 g granulated sugar

2 large eggs, lightly beaten

1½ tsp baking soda

1 tsp pure vanilla extract

3 cups/255 g rolled oats

1½ cups/255 g milk chocolate chips

Heat the oven to 350°F/180°C. Line two baking sheets with parchment paper.

In a large bowl, using an electric mixer, beat together the butter, peanut butter, and both sugars on medium-high speed. Add the eggs, baking soda, and vanilla and beat well to combine. Fold in the oats and chocolate chips and stir until incorporated.

Using a small scoop or a teaspoon, scoop out balls of dough and drop them on the prepared baking sheets about 2 in/5 cm apart.

Bake until the cookies are lightly browned, 12 to 14 minutes. Remove from the oven and cool on the baking sheets for 5 minutes, then transfer the cookies to a wire rack to cool completely.

Store in an airtight container at room temperature for up to 1 week.

Chewy Cinnamon-Molasses Cookies

MAKES 24 COOKIES

There's a cookie shop in my hometown of Sebastopol, California, that sells rows of all kinds of cookies. Their wonderful smell entices passersby to step off Main Street into the little storefront to peruse the freshly baked cookies and pastries—in truth, it's quite hard to resist. My particular favorite, which I've been eating since high school, are the chewy cinnamon-spiked cookies. This recipe is my version of that beloved standard, made without wheat flour.

4 tbsp/55 g unsalted butter, melted and cooled

½ cup/50 g packed light or dark brown sugar

2 tbsp molasses

1 large egg

2 cups/240 g ground almonds

½ tsp baking soda

1 tbsp ground cinnamon

¼ tsp ground cloves

¼ tsp ground ginger

⅛ tsp salt

1 tbsp granulated sugar

Heat the oven to 350°F/180°C. Line two baking sheets with parchment paper. Fill a small ramekin with water.

In a large bowl, whisk the butter with the brown sugar, molasses, and egg. In another bowl, whisk together the ground almonds, baking soda, cinnamon, cloves, ginger, and salt. Add the dry mixture to the butter-molasses mixture and stir well to combine (the dough will be sticky).

With a teaspoon or your fingers, scoop out walnut-size portions of dough. Dampen your hands, then roll the dough portions into balls. Place them on the prepared baking sheets about 1 in/2.5 cm apart. Gently press the cookies with a fork dipped in water to flatten. Sprinkle with the granulated sugar.

Bake until the cookies are set and slightly firm to the touch, 10 to 12 minutes. Remove from the oven and cool on the baking sheets for 5 minutes, then transfer the cookies to a wire rack to cool completely.

Store in an airtight container at room temperature for up to 1 week.

Oat-Maple Cookies

MAKES 24 COOKIES

A friend of mine calls these "make everything better cookies," and indeed they might do just that. Sweet butter married with chewy, wholesome oats touched with ginger and maple syrup create a toothsome sweet that never fails to please. If you prefer thin cookies, bake the dough immediately after mixing. For thicker, chewier cookies, chill the dough for at least an hour.

½ cup/115 g unsalted butter,
at room temperature

⅔ cup/165 ml maple syrup

1 large egg

3½ cups/300 g rolled oats

½ tsp baking powder

½ tsp baking soda

½ tsp salt

½ cup/85 g finely chopped dried apricots

3 tbsp chopped fresh ginger

½ cup/60 g chopped walnuts

Heat the oven to 350°F/180°C. Line two baking sheets with parchment paper.

In a large bowl, using an electric mixer, cream the butter until fluffy. Add the maple syrup and beat until well incorporated; add the egg and beat well to combine (the mixture may look curdled and thin).

In the bowl of a food processor fitted with a steel blade, grind 1½ cups/ 125 g of the rolled oats until fine. Place in a medium bowl and add the baking powder, baking soda, salt, apricots, and ginger. Whisk to combine.

Add the dry mixture to the wet mixture and stir to combine. Add the remaining 2 cups/175 g rolled oats and the walnuts. Stir to incorporate.

With a small scoop or a teaspoon, scoop out balls of dough (the mixture will be wet). Dampen your hands, then squeeze and roll the dough into balls. Place them on the prepared baking sheets about 1 in/2.5 cm apart.

Bake until the cookies are set and lightly browned, about 15 minutes. Remove from the oven and cool on the baking sheets for 2 minutes, then transfer the cookies to a wire rack to cool completely.

Store in an airtight container at room temperature for up to 1 week.

Peanut Butter Cookies

MAKES ABOUT 30 COOKIES

A peanut-y riff on Almond Butter–Chocolate Chip Cookies (page 86), these are creamy with peanut butter, crunchy with chopped peanuts, and finished with a little sea salt and sugar just before baking. You can add chocolate chips if you like, or, instead of the peanut butter, experiment with an equivalent amount of another nut butter such as hazelnut or cashew or even sunflower seed butter.

1 cup/255 g creamy peanut butter

1 cup/200 g packed dark brown sugar

1 large egg

1 tsp baking soda

1 tsp pure vanilla extract

¼ cup/35 g chopped peanuts

1 tsp salt

1 tbsp granulated sugar

Heat the oven to 350°F/180°C. Line two baking sheets with parchment paper.

In a large bowl, stir together the peanut butter and brown sugar until well combined. Add the egg, baking soda, vanilla, and chopped peanuts and mix well.

Using a teaspoon, scoop out walnut-size portions of dough and roll into balls. Place them on the prepared baking sheets about 1 in/2.5 cm apart. Gently press the cookies with a fork and sprinkle evenly with the salt and sugar.

Bake until the cookies are lightly browned, 10 to 12 minutes. Remove from the oven and cool for 5 minutes on wire racks before consuming.

Store in an airtight container at room temperature for up to 1 week.

Banana-Coconut Cookies

MAKES 20 TO 30 COOKIES
(depending on the size of the bananas)

Bananas are sweet enough on their own that no additional sugar is needed in these hearty little cookies. I like them for breakfast when I'm running out the door. If you have bananas that have become overripe and you have no plans to eat them immediately, remove their skins, place the fruit in a plastic bag, and freeze until ready to make this recipe (bananas will need to rest about a half hour at room temperature before mashing).

3 large, very ripe bananas, mashed

¼ cup/60 ml extra-virgin coconut oil (liquid) or vegetable oil

1½ cups/125 g rolled oats

½ cup/60 g ground almonds

1 tsp baking powder

½ tsp ground cinnamon

½ tsp salt

1 cup/120 g chopped walnuts

⅔ cup/50 g unsweetened flaked coconut

Heat the oven to 350°F/180°C. Line two baking sheets with parchment paper.

In a large bowl, stir together the bananas and coconut oil. In another bowl, whisk together the oats, ground almonds, baking powder, cinnamon, and salt. Add the dry ingredients to the wet ingredients and stir to combine. Stir in the walnuts and coconut.

Drop by the teaspoon onto the prepared baking sheets. Bake until the cookies are very lightly browned, about 20 minutes. Remove from the oven and cool on the baking sheets for about 5 minutes then transfer the cookies to a wire rack to cool completely.

Store in an airtight container at room temperature for up to 1 week.

Sesame-Tahini Cookies

MAKES 24 COOKIES

Though tahini is most often used in savory dishes such as hummus or dressings, it is a wonderful addition to baked goods and imparts a halvah-like flavor. I love these little, simple cookies just as they are, but dipping them in melted, bittersweet chocolate would be lovely as well. Serve with mint tea or strong coffee.

1 cup/145 g sesame tahini

¼ cup plus 1 tbsp/110 g honey

1 large egg

½ tsp pure vanilla extract

½ cup/100 g granulated sugar

¼ cup/35 g sesame seeds

¼ cup/50 g raw or coarse sugar, such as turbinado

Heat the oven to 350°F/180°C. Line two baking sheets with parchment paper.

In a large bowl, using an electric mixer, beat together the tahini, honey, egg, and vanilla on medium speed. Add the granulated sugar and beat well to combine. Place the sesame seeds and coarse sugar in separate bowls.

Using a teaspoon, scoop out walnut-size portions of dough and roll into balls, then roll each in the sesame seeds and sugar. Place on the prepared baking sheets.

Bake until the cookies are very lightly browned, about 10 minutes. Remove from the oven and cool on the baking sheet for 5 minutes, then place on a wire rack to cool completely.

Store in an airtight container at room temperature for up to 1 week.

Pignoli (Pine Nut) Cookies

MAKES 36 COOKIES

Toasting the pine nuts before incorporating them into the batter brings out their deep, unique flavor. (Pine nuts may be toasted in a dry skillet placed over a medium-high flame for 3 to 5 minutes, until very lightly browned.)

14 oz/400 g Almond Paste (page 57)
1 cup/100 g confectioners' sugar, sifted
½ cup/50 g granulated sugar
¼ tsp salt
2 egg whites
2 tbsp honey
¼ cup/30 g pine nuts, toasted

Position the racks in the upper and lower thirds of the oven and heat the oven to 350°F/180°C. Line two baking sheets with parchment paper.

Pulse the almond paste in the bowl of a food processor fitted with a steel blade until broken up into small pieces, then add both sugars and the salt and continue to pulse until finely ground, about 1 minute.

Put the almond mixture in a large bowl and add the egg whites and honey. Using an electric mixer beat on medium-high speed until smooth, about 5 minutes (the batter will be very thick).

Using a teaspoon, spoon 1½-in/4-cm rounds onto the prepared baking sheets about 1 in/2.5 cm apart. Gently press the pine nuts liberally into the tops of the cookies to flatten slightly.

Bake, switching the position of the sheets halfway through baking, until the cookies are golden, 12 to 15 minutes total. Slide the cookies, still on the parchment paper, onto wire racks to cool completely. When fully cooled, peel the cookies from the paper. Repeat with the remaining batter.

Store in an airtight container at room temperature for up to 5 days.

Salt-Dusted Lavender-Lemon Cookies

MAKES 24 COOKIES

By now it's probably clear that I love baked goods with a hint of salt, and this recipe is yet another example. Rich with butter, the dough benefits from resting and chilling in the fridge before baking. The blend of lavender and lemon produces a fresh flavor combination that makes these cookies really something special. Note that the cookies are quite delicate and should be consumed within a few days of baking. Food-safe lavender may be bought at many organic markets or online.

¾ cup/60 g whole rolled oats

½ cup/55 g whole raw almonds

3 tbsp cornstarch

2 tbsp sugar

2 tbsp dried lavender

1 ½ tsp salt

½ tsp baking soda

½ cup/115 g chilled unsalted butter, cut into about 8 pieces

Grated zest of 1 large organic lemon, plus 1 tbsp fresh lemon juice

2 tbsp honey

Heat the oven to 350°F/180°C. Line two baking sheets with parchment paper.

In the bowl of a food processor fitted with a steel blade, process the rolled oats and almonds until finely ground. Add the cornstarch, sugar, lavender, ½ tsp of the salt, and the baking soda and pulse until combined.

continued

Add the butter and lemon zest. Pulse until the mixture forms a coarse meal. Add the honey and lemon juice. Pulse until the mixture forms a soft dough. Form the dough into a log; roll and pat the log until it is about 2 in/5 cm in diameter. Wrap in plastic wrap and let rest in the refrigerator for at least 30 minutes. Remove from the fridge and slice into ¼-in/6-mm rounds and place on the prepared baking sheets about ½ in/12 mm apart. Sprinkle with the remaining 1 tsp salt.

Bake until the cookies are light brown around the edges, 9 to 11 minutes. Remove from the oven and cool on the baking sheets for 5 minutes, then transfer the cookies to a wire rack to cool completely, about 15 minutes. The cookies will be very delicate but will firm up as they cool.

The cookies are best eaten within a day or two but may be stored in an airtight container at room temperature for up to 3 days.

Lemon Meringues

MAKES ABOUT 24 COOKIES

"Sunshine cookies" might be another name for these simple, lemony meringues that bake slowly at low heat until they turn crisp and chewy all at once. Another citrus zest—such as lime, blood orange, or grapefruit—may be substituted for the lemon.

2 egg whites

⅛ tsp salt

⅔ cup/130 g sugar

1 tsp grated zest from 1 organic lemon

1 tsp pure vanilla extract

Position the racks in the center and upper third of the oven and heat the oven to 200°F/95°C. Line 2 baking sheets with parchment paper.

Place the egg whites and salt in a large bowl. Using an electric mixer, beat on medium speed until foamy. Increase the speed to medium-high and slowly sprinkle in the sugar, 1 tbsp at a time. Beat until the egg whites are thick, glossy, and hold stiff peaks. Gently fold in the lemon zest and vanilla with a rubber spatula.

Using a teaspoon, gently scoop and drop the batter onto the prepared baking sheets about 1 in/2.5 cm apart.

Bake until the cookies are firm, about 2 hours. Meringues should be fairly dry and not sticky. Remove from the oven and carefully peel the cookies from the parchment paper. Cool on a wire rack or plate until the cookies reach room temperature.

Store in an airtight container at room temperature for up to 1 week.

Salted Rosemary Shortbread

MAKES ABOUT 12 COOKIES

Shortbread cookies traditionally were made in Scotland with oat or brown rice flour, though more contemporary versions call for all-purpose flour. But I love the texture of oat flour and it works so well in this recipe: The cookies are a bit crumbly but still substantial, and the hazelnuts add a graham cracker–like note in counterpoint to the oats. To make a plainer cookie, omit the rosemary and dust with granulated sugar rather than salt before baking.

3 cups/255 g rolled oats

Scant 1 cup/115 g raw hazelnuts

1 tsp salt

1 cup/115 g unsalted butter, at room temperature

½ cup/100 g sugar plus ½ tsp

1 tbsp dried rosemary

Heat the oven to 325°F/165°C. Butter a 9-in/23-cm tart pan with a removable bottom (alternatively, use a well-buttered square pan that is 8 by 8 in/20 by 20 cm).

In the bowl of a food processor fitted with a steel blade, process the rolled oats and hazelnuts until finely ground. Add ¼ tsp of the salt.

In a large bowl, using an electric mixer, cream the butter and ½ cup/100 g sugar on medium-high speed until fluffy. Add the oat mixture to the butter mixture along with the dried rosemary and, using a rubber spatula, gently fold them together until a lumpy, dry dough forms. Press the dough into the prepared pan.

Bake until the dough is set and lightly browned, 55 to 60 minutes. Remove from the oven, sprinkle with the remaining ¾ tsp salt plus the remaining ½ tsp sugar, and cool in the pan for about 10 minutes. Using a butter knife, cut the cookies into 12 wedges in the pan. Put the pan on a wire rack and allow it to cool completely before removing the pieces of shortbread.

Store in an airtight container at room temperature for up to 5 days.

Double Chocolate Brownies

MAKES ABOUT 16 BROWNIES

Because these brownies lack flour, they are more gooey than a traditional brownie, but I like them for that. It's best to let the brownies rest for a few hours after baking—even overnight—as the longer they sit, the firmer they become. The finished product is fudgy and smooth from the melted chocolate. Cut the brownies into small portions as they are very rich.

5 oz/140 g semisweet chocolate
½ cup/155 g unsalted butter
1¼ cups/250 g packed light or dark brown sugar
3 large eggs, lightly beaten
½ cup/50 g unsweetened cocoa powder
¼ tsp salt
1½ tsp pure vanilla extract

Heat the oven to 350°F/180°C. Line an 8-by-8-in/20-by-20-cm square pan with aluminum foil, then lightly grease the foil with vegetable oil.

In a heatproof bowl set over simmering water, melt the chocolate and butter, stirring until smooth. Remove from the heat and transfer to a large bowl; add the brown sugar, eggs, cocoa powder, salt, and vanilla. Stir well to combine. Spread the batter in the pan, smooth with a rubber spatula. Bake until the brownies are dry on top and almost firm to the touch, about 40 minutes. Remove from the oven and cool in the pan for 1 hour.

Gently lift the foil out from the pan after cooling to remove the brownies. Place on a cutting board and refrigerate for up to 1 hour to fully set the brownies. Remove from the fridge and, using a serrated knife, cut into 16 brownies. Serve at room temperature.

Store in an airtight container at room temperature for up to 1 week.

Peanut Butter and Jelly Bars

MAKES 12 TO 16 BARS

Not like the sandwich, exactly, but reminiscent of it, these tidy little bars pack up well and are sure to please. Naturally sweetened with honey, they comprise just a few ingredients you're likely to have readily available.

1 cup/255 g creamy peanut butter

⅓ cup/115 g honey

1 large egg, lightly beaten

½ tsp baking soda

¼ tsp salt

½ cup/50 g jam or jelly of choice

Heat the oven to 350°F/180°C. Lightly grease an 8-by-8-in/20-by-20-cm square pan with vegetable oil.

In a small bowl, mix the peanut butter, honey, egg, baking soda, and salt until well combined.

Pour the batter into the prepared pan and smooth the top with a rubber spatula. Evenly spread the jam over the top of the batter and smooth or decoratively swirl with the spatula.

Bake until the batter is set and a tester inserted into the center comes out clean, 20 to 25 minutes. Remove from the oven and cool completely in the pan before cutting into squares.

Store in an airtight container at room temperature for up to 3 days.

Oatie Squares

MAKES ABOUT 10 SQUARES

One note: These squares are very delicate once baked, so be patient when you extricate them from the pan. Still, the reward is worth it.
You can add a handful of raisins or dried cranberries to make a more traditional kind of granola bar, and I like to use the baked oats as a base for an ice cream sundae or alongside roasted fruit. Good-quality butter makes all the difference here, so splurge on your favorite organic or local brand to really up the flavor potential.

¾ cup/170 g unsalted butter

½ cup/100 g sugar

½ tsp pure vanilla extract

3 cups/255 g rolled oats

2 oz/55 g semisweet chocolate, melted

Heat the oven to 350°F/180°C. Line an 8-by-8-in/20-by-20-cm square baking pan with parchment paper and lightly grease bottom and sides with vegetable oil.

In a saucepan, melt the butter over medium heat. Remove from the heat and let cool slightly. Add the sugar, vanilla, and rolled oats and stir well to combine. Pour the mixture into the prepared pan and press into an even layer.

Bake until the surface is lightly browned and the oats are slightly caramelized, about 30 minutes.

Remove from the oven and drizzle with the melted chocolate. Gently lift the parchment and baked oats from the pan and cut into squares while still warm. Let cool to room temperature before serving.

The squares are best eaten the day they are made, but can be stored in an airtight container for up to 3 days.

Pumpkin Bread

SERVES 10

For this lightly sweetened, maple-scented loaf, scattering sliced almonds or pumpkin seeds across the top of the batter makes for a nice presentation and adds a welcome, extra layer of texture. It's a luscious late-morning snack, topped with melted butter, or partner to tea in the afternoon, especially on cool, windy fall days.

2/3 cup/170 g pumpkin purée

1 cup/120 g ground almonds

1/2 cup/120 ml maple syrup

2 large eggs, lightly beaten

1 tsp ground cinnamon

1/2 tsp ground cloves

1 tsp pure vanilla extract

1/4 tsp sea salt

1 tsp baking soda

1/4 cup/30 g chopped walnuts
(optional)

1/4 cup/45 g semisweet chocolate chips
(optional)

1/4 cup/25 g sliced almonds

Heat the oven to 350°F/180°C. Grease a 9-by-5-in/23-by-13-cm loaf pan with vegetable oil.

Combine the pumpkin purée, ground almonds, maple syrup, eggs, cinnamon, cloves, vanilla, salt, and baking soda together in a medium bowl, and stir well until a smooth batter forms. Stir in the chopped walnuts and chocolate chips (if using). Pour the batter into the prepared pan and scatter the sliced almonds evenly over the top.

Bake until the loaf is puffed and slightly browned and a tester inserted into the middle comes out clean, 35 to 40 minutes. Remove from the oven and cool in the pan for 15 minutes before turning out onto a wire rack to cool completely.

Store tightly wrapped in plastic wrap in the fridge for up to 1 week.

Banana-Cocoa Muffins

MAKES 12 MUFFINS

A combination of mashed bananas, ground hazelnuts, and oats makes up the base for these cocoa-infused muffins sweetened with maple syrup (try an equivalent amount of honey if that's more to your taste). They are ideal as part of a breakfast or as a mid-morning snack—healthful-ish, but never boring, thanks to the chocolate.

2 large eggs

½ cup/120 ml maple syrup

¼ cup/60 ml extra-virgin olive oil

2 very ripe bananas, mashed

½ cup/60 g ground hazelnuts

½ cup/40 g ground rolled oats

½ cup/50 g unsweetened cocoa powder

1¼ tsp baking powder

½ tsp salt

½ tsp ground cinnamon

Heat the oven to 350°F/180°C. Line a 12-cup cupcake tin with cupcake liners.

In a medium bowl, whisk together the eggs, maple syrup, and olive oil until well combined. Add the bananas and stir well. In a large bowl, whisk together the ground hazelnuts, oats, cocoa powder, baking powder, salt, and cinnamon.

Fold the wet ingredients into the dry ingredients and stir well to combine. Pour the batter into the prepared tin.

Bake until the muffins are lightly browned and a skewer inserted into the centers comes out clean, about 30 minutes. Remove from the oven and cool for 10 minutes in the tin on a wire rack before turning out onto the rack to cool completely.

Store in an airtight container at room temperature for up to 5 days.

Honeyed Blueberry Cakes

MAKES 12 CAKES

These cakes are lightly sweet, calling upon honey and blueberries to impart flavor. They are wonderful as part of a brunch spread— or with a late cup of coffee—but served with vanilla ice cream make a rustic finish to a simple dinner.

1 cup/120 g ground almonds

1 cup/140 g cornmeal

2 tsp baking powder

½ tsp baking soda

1 tsp salt

4 tbsp/55 g unsalted butter, melted and cooled

1 large egg, lightly beaten

1 cup/240 ml whole milk

¼ cup/60 ml honey

1 cup/110 g fresh or frozen blueberries

Heat the oven to 350°F/180°C. Line a 12-cup cupcake tin with cupcake liners.

In a large bowl, stir together the ground almonds, cornmeal, baking powder, baking soda, and salt. In a separate bowl, whisk together the melted butter, egg, milk, and honey.

Add the wet ingredients to the dry ingredients and mix just until combined. Stir in the blueberries. Add the batter to the prepared tin, filling the cups evenly.

Bake the cakes until a skewer inserted into the centers comes out clean, 20 to 25 minutes. Remove from the oven and place on a wire rack. Cool completely in the tin before removing.

Store in an airtight container at room temperature for up to 5 days.

Dried Fruit and Nut "Truffles"

MAKES ABOUT 36 COOKIES

These cookies couldn't be easier to make, and I encourage you to experiment with different dried fruits of your choice, substituted in equivalent amounts. The chocolate coating may be left off if you are pressed for time, but I think it elevates these humble little raw "truffles" into something sublime. Otherwise, dust lightly with more confectioners' sugar just before serving.

1 cup/120 g chopped walnuts

8 oz/230 g dried cherries

8 oz/230 g dried Turkish figs

8 oz/230 g dried apricots

4 oz/115 g dried cranberries

1 to 2 tbsp fresh orange juice

½ cup/50 g confectioners' sugar

8 oz/230 g bittersweet or semisweet chocolate, coarsely chopped or as chips

Put the walnuts in the bowl of a food processor fitted with a steel blade and process until finely ground. Pour the ground walnuts into a large bowl.

Clean and dry the bowl of the food processor and fill it with the dried cherries, figs, apricots, and cranberries. Pulse the machine to chop the fruit finely (make sure the fruit doesn't turn gummy).

Add the fruit to the walnuts and stir to mix well. Add 1 tbsp of the orange juice and stir to combine (add more if needed, to help the mixture hold together in a sticky dough).

continued

Put the confectioners' sugar in a small bowl. Scoop out 1-tsp balls of the fruit-nut mixture. Shape each into a ball, roll each ball lightly in confectioners' sugar to coat, and place on a baking sheet. Let the balls stand at room temperature, uncovered, for 24 hours.

When ready for dipping, line a baking sheet with parchment paper. Melt the chocolate in a metal bowl set over a pot of simmering water. Using a toothpick, spear each ball and dip it halfway in the chocolate. Place the ball, plain-side down, on the prepared sheet and let stand until the chocolate has cooled.

Store in an airtight container at room temperature or in the fridge for up to 1 week.

Puddings, Tarts, and Other Delights

Fluffy puddings, baked custard, berry crumbles and trifles, all kinds of baked fruit, almond-coconut crusts bolstering a lemon or coconut-milk filling and topped with fruit—this section is full of fresh flavors and ingredients. And it just might be my favorite chapter in this cookbook.

It's partly because of the variety. I've tried to strike a balance here between recipes that are a bit more sophisticated, such as Salted Caramel Pots de Crème or a velvety chocolate cream pie with a hazelnut-cocoa crust, and those that appeal to the craving for simplicity we all have, like baked apples with cinnamon cream or a fruit crumble topped with a mixture of rolled oats and brown sugar.

Many of these recipes call for not much more than a trip to the farmers' market to pick up fresh seasonal fruit and then roasting it in the oven (serving with dollops of homemade crème fraîche ups the ante). For days when whipping egg whites seems like too much effort, made-from-scratch milk chocolate pudding satisfies the yen for something sweet. Stone fruit baked long and slow until the oven's heat brings out its inherent sweetness (and then paired with a scoop of mascarpone cheese drizzled with honey) is a wonderfully simple summer treat. For the hottest days of August, a buttermilk panna cotta requires only a brief use of the stove and time in the fridge to chill into a refreshingly unique dessert.

And on days when some time in the kitchen seems like just the thing, try a strawberries-and-cream trifle with a flourless sponge cake as its base or a creamy citrus-infused flan (a baked Spanish custard) that needs no further adornment. A cheesecake topped with Meyer lemon curd, so rich and smooth you'll never miss the crust, is an awfully effective way to show-case your flourless-dessert-making skills.

But this section might just be my favorite because these desserts are simply so good. They are not fussy, even if a few might be slightly more time-consuming, and many are what I would describe as comforting (the butterscotch pudding in particular is hard not to spoon straight from the pot). They certainly will create happiness when you bring them to the table.

Milk Chocolate Pudding

SERVES 4

This pudding could hardly be simpler to make: whisk cocoa powder, cornstarch, a little sugar, milk, heavy cream, and milk chocolate together in a pot until thick and bubbling. Whipped cream to finish is a must. If you have some strawberries from the farmers' market, those probably would taste quite divine sliced and strewn across the top—if you're into that kind of thing (I certainly am).

2 tbsp sugar

2 tbsp cornstarch

2 tbsp unsweetened cocoa powder

¼ tsp salt

1½ cups/360 ml whole milk

½ cup/120 ml heavy cream

4 oz/115 g good-quality milk chocolate, chopped

1 tsp pure vanilla extract

Lightly sweetened whipped cream for accompaniment

In a heavy saucepan, whisk together the sugar, cornstarch, cocoa powder, and salt, then whisk in the milk and heavy cream. Bring the mixture to a boil over moderately high heat, whisking constantly, then boil, whisking, for 2 minutes (the mixture should be thick). Remove from the heat.

Stir in the chocolate and vanilla and whisk until smooth. Transfer to a bowl and chill until cold, at least 2 hours (the surface may be covered with waxed paper or plastic wrap to prevent a skin from forming).

Serve immediately, with lightly sweetened whipped cream, or store in the refrigerator, covered, for up to 3 days.

Butterscotch Pudding with Banana Whipped Cream

SERVES 4

If roasted bananas aren't to your taste, whip the cream without them and add a dash of vanilla extract instead.

BUTTERSCOTCH PUDDING

½ cup/100 g packed dark brown sugar

2 tbsp plus 1 tsp cornstarch

½ tsp salt

1½ cups/360 ml whole milk

½ cup/120 ml heavy cream

2 tbsp unsalted butter

1 tsp pure vanilla extract

BANANA WHIPPED CREAM

2 tbsp unsalted butter

2 tbsp packed dark or light brown sugar

1 ripe banana, peeled and sliced into ½-in/12-mm rounds

1 cup/240 ml heavy cream

To make the pudding: In a medium saucepan, whisk together the brown sugar, cornstarch, and salt, then whisk in the milk and heavy cream. Bring the mixture to a boil over medium heat, whisking frequently. Continue to whisk for 1 minute, then remove from the heat and stir in the butter and vanilla until well combined. Pour into a bowl and cover the surface with waxed paper or plastic wrap. Chill until cold, at least 2 hours.

To make the whipped cream: Put the butter and brown sugar in a frying pan over medium heat. Stirring continuously, cook until the butter and sugar have melted together.

Add the banana slices and cook for 1 minute until the edges are slightly caramelized. Turn the slices over and cook for 1 minute more. Pour the bananas onto a large cutting board, let cool slightly, then coarsely chop.

In a large bowl, using an electric mixer, whip the heavy cream on medium-high speed just until soft peaks form. Gently fold in the banana pieces until just incorporated.

Top each portion of pudding with a generous spoonful of the whipped cream to serve.

Bourbon–Arborio Rice Pudding

SERVES 6

My husband dearly loves rice pudding—so much so that he will spoon it up straight from the pan while I hover in the background entreating him to use a bowl. Still, no matter what way you eat it, this pudding tastes of pure comfort. Here, I add fresh ginger to give a bit of bite that contrasts with the creamy, soft, coconut-infused rice. A touch of bourbon adds an extra zing, too. I use margarine here to keep the recipe dairy-free.

2 cups/480 ml full-fat coconut milk

3 cups/720 ml water

½ cup/100 g Arborio rice

⅓ cup/65 g granulated sugar

2 tbsp packed dark brown sugar

1 tbsp chopped fresh ginger

1 tsp bourbon (optional)

½ cup/85 g golden raisins

2 tbsp nondairy margarine,
such as Earth Balance (optional)

Position the rack in the center of the oven and heat the oven to 325°F/165°C. Lightly grease an 8-by-8-in/20-by-20-cm square pan with vegetable oil.

Add the coconut milk, water, rice, both sugars, ginger, and bourbon (if using) to the pan and stir gently to combine.

Bake for 2 hours, stirring at 30 minute intervals. After 2 hours, stir in the raisins and bake for 30 minutes more without stirring.

Remove the pan from the oven. Skim off and discard the skin from the pudding, then stir in the margarine.

The pudding can be eaten at room temperature or chilled at least 30 minutes before serving. The pudding is best served the day it's made, but it can be made up to 1 day in advance before serving.

Indian Pudding

SERVES 10

Good things come to those who wait, and this traditional New England pudding is no exception. Ingredients come together easily and then the dish bakes slowly for a few hours. You'll know it's done when the pudding's edges just barely pull away from the pan and the middle is set but still slightly jiggly. It smells of cinnamon and molasses, corn and ginger—in other words, like fall. Eat hot with vanilla ice cream or a generous spoonful of Greek yogurt.

4 cups/960 ml whole milk

1 cup/140 g cornmeal

¼ cup/55 g unsalted butter, cut into pieces

2 large eggs, lightly beaten

¼ cup/60 ml maple syrup

⅔ cup/180 ml molasses

¾ tsp salt

1 tsp ground cinnamon

½ tsp ground ginger

¼ tsp ground cloves

⅛ tsp ground nutmeg

Heat the oven to 325°F/165°C. Lightly butter an 8-by-10-in/20-by-25-cm baking dish.

In a heavy saucepan, bring the milk to a boil over medium heat. Add the cornmeal gradually, whisking constantly and vigorously. As the mixture thickens, remove from the heat and stir in the butter until melted. Set aside to cool.

When the mixture is cool, stir in the eggs, maple syrup, molasses, salt, cinnamon, ginger, cloves, and nutmeg. Mix well to combine.

Pour into the prepared baking dish and bake until the pudding starts to pull away from the sides of the pan and is set in the center (it will be a little wobbly), about 2 hours.

Remove from the oven and serve hot or warm.

Pumpkin Pie Puddings

SERVES 6

The absence of a crust is not even a remote issue here; don't most of us really crave the spice-kissed pumpkin filling in a traditional pie rather than its crust? I think so, anyway. These puddings more than satisfy that desire. Try coconut milk in place of the whole milk if you cannot have dairy—or just like the flavor—for a gentle twist on a familiar favorite.

One 15-oz/450-g can pumpkin purée

½ cup/120 ml coconut milk or whole milk

4 large eggs, slightly beaten

¼ cup/60 ml maple syrup

1 tbsp bourbon (optional)

2 tsp pure vanilla extract

½ tsp salt

1 tsp ground cinnamon

½ tsp ground ginger

¼ tsp ground nutmeg

Heat the oven to 350°F/180°C. Lightly grease six ½-cup/120-ml ramekins with vegetable oil.

In a large bowl, whisk together the pumpkin purée, milk, eggs, maple syrup, bourbon (if using), and vanilla. In a small bowl, whisk together the salt, cinnamon, ginger, and nutmeg. Add the spice mixture to the pumpkin mixture and whisk well to combine.

Pour the mixture into the prepared ramekins, dividing it evenly. Place the ramekins on a baking sheet and bake until a knife inserted in the middle of a pudding comes out clean, about 40 minutes.

Remove from the oven, transfer the ramekins to a wire rack, and let cool for 15 minutes. Chill the puddings, lightly covered with plastic wrap, in the fridge for at least 2 hours before serving.

Lemon Pudding Cake

SERVES 6

Not quite a cake and not quite a pudding, this dessert is an unexpected combination of both. A pillowy layer of cake—really, a flourless lemon-infused sponge—floats above a tart sea of incredibly spoonable lemon pudding. An elegant finish to a dinner party, this cake-pudding is easy enough to put together on a weeknight for a last-minute sweet treat.

4 tbsp/25 g cornstarch

¼ tsp salt

½ cup plus 2 tbsp/125 g granulated sugar

3 large eggs, separated, at room temperature

1⅓ cups/315 ml whole milk

Grated zest of 1 organic lemon, plus juice of 2 lemons

1 tsp pure vanilla extract

¼ cup/60 ml honey

1 to 2 tbsp confectioners' sugar

Heat the oven to 350°F/180°C. Butter a 1½-qt/1.5-L heatproof gratin dish or other shallow baking dish.

In a large bowl, whisk together the cornstarch, salt, and sugar.

In a small bowl, whisk together the egg yolks, milk, lemon zest, lemon juice, and vanilla. Add to the cornstarch mixture, whisking until just combined.

In another large bowl, using an electric mixer, beat the egg whites on high speed until they hold soft peaks. Beat in the honey a little at a time, and continue to beat until the whites hold stiff, glossy peaks. Whisk about one-quarter of the whites into the lemon batter to lighten, then gently but thoroughly fold in the remaining whites (the batter will be thin).

Pour into the prepared dish, and set the dish in a large roasting pan. Fill the roasting pan with hot water until it comes about halfway up the sides of the baking dish to make a water bath. Carefully place the roasting pan in the oven and bake until the cake is puffed and golden, 45 to 50 minutes.

Remove from the oven and transfer the baking dish to a wire rack to cool slightly. Sprinkle the surface with the confectioners' sugar.

Serve warm or at room temperature, spooning generous portions of the pudding cake into dessert bowls.

Buttermilk-Nutmeg Panna Cotta

SERVES 6

Panna cotta is an Italian dessert typically served with fresh fruit or chocolate or caramel sauce. I've added a note of nutmeg as well as a slight undertone of coffee in a nod to the dessert's origins (Italians being known for making terrific espresso). I'd argue that portions need no accompaniment, although blackberries would be very nice (not to mention a drizzle of salted caramel sauce—see page 20). Panna cotta is lovely for hot days when you can't bear the thought of turning on the oven. If you avoid dairy, substitute unsweetened almond milk for the buttermilk and cream.

1²⁄₃ cups/400 ml buttermilk

1½ tsp unflavored gelatin powder

1 cup/240 ml heavy cream

½ cup/100 g sugar

1 tsp ground nutmeg

1 tsp pure vanilla extract

1 tsp instant espresso powder

Have a glass loaf pan or six ½-cup/120-ml ramekins ready.

Place 1 cup/240 ml of the buttermilk in a heatproof bowl. Sprinkle the gelatin across the surface and let sit for 5 minutes.

Put ²⁄₃ cup/160 ml of the heavy cream and the sugar in a small pan and bring to a boil over medium-high heat. Remove from the heat and pour over the buttermilk mixture. Place the bowl over a pan of simmering water and stir until the gelatin is completely dissolved, 5 to 10 minutes.

Remove the bowl from the heat and stir in the remaining buttermilk, the remaining heavy cream, nutmeg, vanilla, and espresso powder. Stir well to combine, then pour into the loaf pan or ramekins. Cover with plastic wrap and refrigerate until set, about 4 hours.

Run the tip of a thin knife around the edges and invert the panna cottas onto a platter, or serve out of the pan.

Maple Mousse

SERVES 10

Not only is a mousse a great make-ahead dessert, a bonus is that it travels well. Though dessert mousses are often made with chocolate, the addition of maple syrup in this version adds a more rustic touch. To garnish, a sprinkling of chopped toasted nuts or shaved bittersweet chocolate would be lovely, though it hardly needs any adornment. This beauty stands on its own.

1 large egg white

¾ cup/180 ml maple syrup

1 cup/240 ml heavy cream

Berries, chopped toasted nuts, or shaved chocolate for garnish (optional)

Have a 1-qt/960-ml heatproof mold or baking dish ready.

Place a large bowl in the freezer. In another large bowl, using an electric mixer, beat the egg white on medium speed until it thickens and begins to hold soft peaks. Slowly pour in the maple syrup and continue to beat on medium speed until it has a thick, meringue-like texture.

Beat the heavy cream in the chilled bowl on medium-high speed until stiff peaks form. Gently fold the beaten cream into the maple syrup mixture, stirring lightly until incorporated and no white streaks remain. Pour into the mold or baking dish and place in the freezer for at least 4 hours.

Thaw in the refrigerator about 30 minutes before serving. Cut the mousse into medium-thick wedges to serve. Garnish with berries, nuts, or chocolate, if desired.

Citrus Flan

SERVES 6

Flan is a smooth, baked egg custard into which myriad flavors
can be incorporated. I've kept things fairly simple here with the inclusion
of orange zest and juice and use heavy cream and half-and-half rather
than the evaporated milk that is sometimes found in other recipes.
I think it makes for a creamier flan overall.

⅓ cup/65 g granulated sugar

2 tbsp packed light or dark brown sugar

2 large eggs

1 cup/240 ml heavy cream

1 cup/240 ml half-and-half

1½ tsp pure vanilla extract

Grated zest plus 1 tsp fresh juice of
1 organic orange

Heat the oven to 325°F/165°C. Have six ½-cup/120-ml ramekins ready.

In a medium bowl, whisk together both sugars and the eggs. Add the
cream, half-and-half, and vanilla and whisk to combine and dissolve the
sugar. Whisk in the orange zest and juice and let sit for a few minutes.

Pour the custard into the ramekins and set the ramekins in a roasting
pan. Pour boiling water into the roasting pan until it reaches a little
more than halfway up the sides of the ramekins.

Carefully place the roasting pan in the oven and bake for 25 minutes,
then rotate the pan so the custards in the back are now in the front.
Bake until the custards are set but their centers still jiggle when nudged
(test one of the ramekins), 20 to 25 minutes longer.

Remove the roasting pan from the oven and let the flans cool in the pan
for 30 minutes. Remove the ramekins from the water bath and cool
completely on a wire rack. Cover with plastic wrap and chill overnight.

Let stand at room temperature for 10 minutes. Gently run a knife
around the edges of each flan and unmold the flans onto plates to serve.

Salted Caramel Pots de Crème

SERVES 6

These little custards are plush and smooth, sending flavors of deep caramelized sugar across your tongue—they are rich, but not overly so. You probably also have most of the ingredients in your fridge right now for a quick pick-me-up dessert. Don't be intimidated by the water bath; it's crucial to ensure even cooking. Save the egg whites to make meringue cookies (see page 102), another flourless treat.

1 cup/200 g sugar
⅓ cup/80 ml water plus ¼ cup/60 ml
1½ cups/360 ml heavy cream
1½ cups/360 ml whole milk
8 egg yolks
1 tsp coarse salt

Heat the oven to 325°F/165°C. Have six ½-cup/120-ml ramekins ready.

In a heavy saucepan, combine the sugar and ⅓ cup/80 ml water, cover, and bring to a boil over medium-high heat. Uncover and cook, without stirring, until the sugar turns golden amber in color, 8 to 12 minutes.

Meanwhile, combine the cream and milk in a large saucepan over medium-high heat and warm until small bubbles appear along the edges of the pan. Remove from the heat.

When the caramel is ready, add the remaining ¼ cup/60 ml water and whisk vigorously until the bubbles subside. Pour the caramel into the hot cream mixture and whisk until well combined. The mixture may bubble up a bit. Remove from the heat and cool for about 10 minutes.

In a large bowl, whisk the egg yolks. Slowly add the caramel mixture to the egg yolks, stirring constantly with a wooden spoon until combined. Strain through a fine-mesh sieve into a bowl.

Pour the custard into the ramekins and set the ramekins in a roasting pan. Pour boiling water into the roasting pan until it reaches a little more than halfway up the sides of the ramekins.

Carefully place the roasting pan in the oven and bake until the edges of the custards are set, 40 to 50 minutes.

Remove the roasting pan from the oven and place on a wire rack to cool for 10 minutes. Remove the ramekins from the water bath and cool on the rack. Sprinkle the salt across the top of the custards.

Refrigerate, lightly covered with plastic wrap, for several hours or overnight until well chilled. Serve chilled.

Chocolate Cream Pie

SERVES 10

I often make a chocolate cream pie for holiday gatherings because it seems to offer just the right amount of decadence to properly celebrate the season. I've come up with a slightly crumbly hazelnut-cocoa crust that is suitably flourless as well as being a wonderful complement to the rich chocolate. Be gentle as you press it into your baking pan, as it may be a bit delicate to work with.

HAZELNUT-COCOA CRUST

2½ cups/390 g whole hazelnuts

¼ cup/30 g sugar

1 tbsp unsweetened cocoa powder

2 tbsp unsalted butter, melted

CHOCOLATE FILLING

⅔ cup/130 g sugar

¼ cup/25 g cornstarch

½ tsp salt

4 egg yolks

3 cups/720 ml whole milk

7 oz/200 g bittersweet chocolate, melted

2 tbsp unsalted butter,
at room temperature

1 tsp pure vanilla extract

Coconut Milk Whipped Cream (recipe follows)
or regular whipped cream for topping

Heat the oven to 350°F/180°C. Have a 9-in/23-cm pie pan ready.

To make the crust: Place the hazelnuts on a rimmed baking sheet. Toast in the oven until the nuts are lightly browned and release a nutty fragrance, about 15 minutes. Remove the hazelnuts from the oven and set aside to cool. When nuts are completely cooled, use your hands to rub off as many of the skins as you can. Don't worry if you can't remove all of the skin; a little bit is OK.

continued

In the bowl of a food processor fitted with a steel blade, process the hazelnuts, sugar, and cocoa powder until fine. Place in a bowl and add the melted butter, stirring to combine. Press the mixture onto the bottom and up the sides of the pie pan. Bake the crust until slightly crisp, about 25 minutes. Remove from the oven and cool on a wire rack.

To make the filling: In a medium, heavy saucepan, whisk together the sugar, cornstarch, salt, and egg yolks until well combined, then add the milk in a steady stream, whisking continuously. Bring to a boil over medium heat, whisking, then decrease the heat and simmer, whisking, for 1 minute more (the filling will be thick).

Force the filling through a fine-mesh sieve into a bowl, then whisk in the chocolate, butter, and vanilla. Cover the surface of the filling with a buttered round of waxed paper and cool completely, about 2 hours.

Spoon the filling into the crust. Chill the pie, loosely covered with plastic wrap, for at least 6 hours. Top with a thick layer of whipped cream.

Use a serrated knife to cut the pie into slices and use a cake server to gently place the slices on plates to serve. Note that the crust will be a little crumbly, so go easy.

COCONUT MILK WHIPPED CREAM
One 13.5-oz/400-ml can full-fat coconut milk
3 tbsp confectioners' sugar
½ tsp pure vanilla extract

Store the can of coconut milk upside down in the refrigerator overnight.

The next morning, turn the can right-side up and open it. Drain the liquid into a separate container and discard.

Place the coconut milk solids in a large bowl and add the confectioners' sugar and vanilla. Beat with an electric mixer on medium-high speed until the mixture resembles whipped cream, about 1 minute.

Use immediately in place of whipped cream as a frosting or as an accompaniment.

Lemon Cream Pie

SERVES 10

The filling for this pie comes together in a snap: heavy cream is boiled with sugar for a few minutes, lemon juice and zest are whisked in, and then it's left to chill in the refrigerator. This wonderfully refreshing filling requires no additional components. The coconut-almond crust is just the thing to bring it all together into a gorgeously bright and unfussy treat.

COCONUT-ALMOND CRUST

1¼ cups/90 g unsweetened flaked coconut

1¼ cups/225 g whole almonds

¼ cup/40 ml oil of choice, such as coconut, vegetable, or olive

3 tbsp honey

LEMON CREAM FILLING

2 cups/480 ml heavy cream

⅔ cup/130 g sugar

Fresh juice of 2 lemons, plus
grated zest of 1 organic lemon

Heat the oven to 350°F/180°C. Have an 8-in/20-cm or 9-in/23-cm tart pan with a removable bottom ready.

To make the crust: Place the coconut and almonds in the bowl of a food processor fitted with a steel blade and process until finely ground. Place the mixture in a large bowl and work in the oil and honey, whisking and blending with a fork until well combined. Press the crust into the tart pan and bake until evenly and lightly browned, 10 to 12 minutes. Remove from the oven and cool completely, at least 1 hour.

To make the filling: In a medium saucepan, bring the cream and sugar to a boil over medium-high heat, stirring to dissolve the sugar. Continue boiling for 5 minutes, watching so it does not boil over. Remove the pan from the heat and stir in the lemon juice and zest.

Pour the filling into the baked crust. Chill in the refrigerator for at least 2 hours before serving.

Cheesecake with Meyer Lemon Curd

SERVES 12

In this crustless cheesecake, smooth mascarpone cheese marries with cream cheese for a creamy, light-tasting dessert. If Meyer lemons are not available for the lemon curd, regular lemons will work instead, but the curd will be a bit tarter than the more mellow lemon flavor imparted by the Meyers.

MASCARPONE CHEESECAKE

20 oz/570 g cream cheese,
at room temperature

8 oz/225 g mascarpone cheese,
at room temperature

¾ cup/150 g sugar

3 large eggs

1 tsp pure vanilla extract

1 tsp fresh juice, plus grated zest from
1 organic lemon

¼ teaspoon salt

MEYER LEMON CURD

3 large eggs

¾ cup/150 g sugar

⅓ cup/75 ml fresh Meyer lemon juice
(from about 2 or 3 lemons),
plus 1 tbsp finely grated zest from
1 organic lemon

4 tbsp/55 g unsalted butter,
cut into small pieces

continued

Heat the oven to 350°F/180°C. Have a 9-in/23-cm springform pan ready.

To make the cheesecake: In a large bowl, using an electric mixer, beat the cream cheese, mascarpone, and sugar on medium-high speed until fluffy, 3 to 5 minutes. Add the eggs, one at a time, beating well after each addition. Add the vanilla, lemon juice, lemon zest, and salt and mix on low speed until combined.

Pour into the pan and bake until the cake is set and puffed around its edges but still trembles slightly when the pan is shaken gently, 45 to 50 minutes. Remove from the oven and cool completely in the pan on a wire rack. Chill, loosely covered with plastic wrap, at least 8 hours.

Meanwhile, make the lemon curd: In a stainless-steel bowl placed over a saucepan of simmering water, whisk together the eggs, sugar, and lemon juice until blended.

Cook, stirring constantly to prevent the mixture from curdling, until it becomes thick, about 10 minutes. Remove from the heat and immediately pour through a fine-mesh strainer into a bowl to remove any lumps, pressing it through if necessary.

Add the butter to the lemon mixture, whisking until the butter has melted. Stir in the lemon zest and cool to room temperature. The lemon curd will continue to thicken as it cools. Cover and refrigerate.

After the cheesecake and curd have chilled for about 8 hours, spread a medium-thick layer of curd over the top of the cake (you will have leftover curd). Keep the cheesecake refrigerated, loosely tented with aluminum foil, until ready to serve. Use a serrated knife to carefully cut slices of the cake.

Store, covered, in the fridge for up to 4 days.

Peach, Lemon, and Rosemary Verrines

SERVES 4

A verrine is a pretty French snack or dessert comprising savory or sweet ingredients layered in a small glass. Here, a purée of peaches is topped by a tart lemon pudding and finished with a bit of whipped cream, aromatic fresh rosemary, and chopped pistachio nuts. Choose your nicest clear glasses to really showcase the eye-catching composition.

LEMON PUDDING

½ cup/100 g sugar

2 tbsp cornstarch

⅛ tsp salt

2 cups/480 ml whole milk

1 tsp grated zest from
1 organic lemon, plus
¼ cup/60 ml fresh lemon juice

2 tbsp unsalted butter,
cut into bits

1 egg yolk

4 ripe peaches, peeled, pitted,
and cut into large chunks

1 cup/240 ml heavy cream

2 tsp fresh rosemary leaves

¼ cup/25 g chopped
pistachio nuts

To make the pudding: In a heavy saucepan, whisk together the sugar, cornstarch, and salt. Add the milk and lemon zest and whisk until smooth. Bring to a boil over medium heat, whisking constantly, then boil, whisking constantly, for 2 minutes.

continued

Remove from the heat and whisk in the lemon juice, butter, and egg yolk. Transfer the pudding to a bowl. (If desired, stir in more lemon juice.) Stir until the butter is melted. Chill the pudding, its surface covered with parchment paper, until thickened, about 2 hours.

Place the peach chunks in a heavy saucepan and cook over medium heat until the peaches are soft, stirring occasionally, for about 10 minutes. The mixture should resemble a purée; you may need to use a wooden spoon to smash and break up any lumps. Remove from the heat and cool, then chill for 2 hours.

Divide the purée evenly between four tall glasses or glass jars. Top with equal amounts of the pudding. Put the filled glasses in the fridge, uncovered, and chill thoroughly until ready to serve.

In a large bowl, using an electric mixer, beat the heavy cream until soft peaks form. Finish each verrine with generous dollops of whipped cream. Garnish with the fresh rosemary leaves and the chopped pistachio nuts before serving.

Strawberries and Cream Trifle

SERVES 12

A trifle—a traditional British dessert—leaves a lot of room for experimentation. The basic structure is as follows: a layer of sponge cake, a layer of fruit preserves, a sprinkling of fresh fruit, and a final layer of custard that is finished off with a good amount of whipped cream (toasted nuts, or chopped cookies such as amaretti, are optional garnishes). I've tried to give a semblance of a recipe here, but certainly play around with different jam/fruit combinations as you like. (Also try folding small chunks of angel food cake and fruit into a few cups of freshly whipped cream for a light and quick dessert.) It's important to note that a trifle needs at least 8 hours to chill before serving, which makes it a wonderful party dessert. A large glass serving bowl or glass trifle dish will best show off the beauty of the contrasting layers.

VANILLA CUSTARD

¼ cup/50 g sugar

2 tbsp plus 2 tsp cornstarch

¼ tsp salt

2 cups/480 ml whole milk

2 egg yolks

1 tbsp butter

½ tsp pure vanilla extract

2 cups/480 ml heavy cream

1 plain Angel Food Cake
(page 29; omit the citrus zest and
juice and the poppy seeds)

2 cups/680 g jam of choice,
such as blackberry, strawberry, or raspberry

1 lb/455 g fresh berries of choice
(often this is the same as the jam),
sliced, if necessary

1 cup/120 g chopped nuts,
such as almonds, pistachios, or walnuts, or
crumbled cookies such as Amaretti (page 79)
or Lemon Meringues (page 102)

To make the custard: In a medium saucepan, whisk together the sugar, cornstarch, and salt. Slowly pour in the milk, whisking constantly to break up any lumps. Bring the mixture to a boil over medium-high heat, whisking occasionally. The mixture will thicken. Remove from the heat when the mixture is thick enough to coat the back of a spoon.

Place the egg yolks in a medium bowl and immediately whisk in about one-third of the hot milk mixture to temper, then pour in the rest of the milk, whisking to combine well. Pour the mixture back into the saucepan and cook over medium-high heat for about 30 seconds. Remove from the heat and whisk in the butter and vanilla.

Return the custard to the bowl and cool to room temperature.

In a large bowl, whip the cream to medium-firm peaks. Cut the angel food cake into pieces so that it will form a flat layer on the bottom (the sponge cake layer) of a large glass bowl or a 3-qt/3-L trifle dish. Spread the jam across the cake layer and top with the fresh berries. Top with the vanilla custard, then finish with a thick layer of whipped cream. Garnish with the nuts or crushed cookies.

Cover the trifle loosely with plastic wrap and chill in the refrigerator for at least 8 hours, or up to 24 hours, to allow the flavors to mingle. Serve straight out of the fridge.

Eton Mess

SERVES 12

This classic British dessert—a mixture of crushed meringue cookies mixed with whipped cream and strawberries—was traditionally served at Eton College's annual cricket match against Harrow School. To play a bit loose with the recipe, try substituting other fruits for the strawberries as you wish; though strawberries are more commonly used, they are by no means absolutely necessary to convey the spirit of this light, summery dessert. Plan to make the meringues a day or two in advance of assembling the final dish as they need to dry out overnight in the oven.

MERINGUES

3 egg whites

¼ tsp cream of tartar

¾ cup/150 g sugar

½ tsp pure vanilla extract

STRAWBERRIES AND CREAM

1 lb/455 g strawberries, tops trimmed

3 tbsp sugar

1 cup/240 ml heavy cream

½ tsp pure vanilla extract

Position the rack in the center of the oven and heat the oven to 200°F/95°C. Line a baking sheet with parchment paper.

To make the meringues: In a large bowl, using an electric mixer, beat the egg whites on medium speed until foamy. Add the cream of tartar and continue to beat the whites until they hold soft peaks. Add the sugar, a little at a time, and continue to beat until the whites hold very stiff peaks. Beat in the vanilla until just incorporated.

Using two tablespoons, place ten equal-size mounds of meringue on the prepared baking sheet, 1 in/2.5 cm apart.

continued

Bake the meringues for 1½ to 1¾ hours, rotating the baking sheet from front to back halfway through the cooking time. The meringues are done when they are pale in color and fairly crisp. Turn off the oven, open the door a crack, and leave the meringues in the oven to finish drying overnight.

To prepare the strawberries and cream: Up to 8 hours ahead of serving, place about one-third of the strawberries in the bowl of a food processor fitted with a steel blade and process until just puréed. Place the purée in a large bowl. Cut the rest of the strawberries into bite-size pieces and add to the purée. Sprinkle 2 tbsp of the sugar over the strawberries and stir to combine.

Just before assembling, place the heavy cream, vanilla, and remaining 1 tbsp sugar in a large bowl. Beat with an electric mixer on high speed until stiff peaks form.

When ready to assemble, break the meringue cookies into bite-size pieces. Gently fold the meringue pieces and the strawberry sauce into the whipped cream.

Place in individual glass bowls, wine glasses, or tall clear drinking glasses and serve immediately.

Mixed Berry Crumble

SERVES 8

Frozen berries work just fine here, though I like to make this in summer when fresh berries are plentiful in the markets or, if I'm lucky enough, I can pick them myself. This recipe can be used as a basic template for making a crumble—you can use any type of fruit you like (apples, peaches, or the classic springtime combination of strawberries and rhubarb come to mind). Just be sure you have enough to make a thick fruit layer to bolster the crisp topping. Serving portions warm, with vanilla ice cream, is a must.

4 cups/570 g berries,
such as blueberries, blackberries,
raspberries, or a combination

4 tsp fresh lemon juice

½ tsp pure vanilla extract

1 cup/100 g packed light or dark brown sugar

½ tsp ground cinnamon

1 cup/85 g whole rolled oats

¼ cup/55 g unsalted butter, at room temperature,
or ½ cup/120 ml olive oil

Vanilla ice cream or plain yogurt
for serving

Heat the oven to 350°F/180°C. Lightly grease a 9-by-12-in/23-by-30.5-cm baking pan.

In a bowl, combine the berries, lemon juice, and vanilla. Toss to combine.

In another bowl, stir together the brown sugar, cinnamon, and rolled oats. Cut in the butter, rubbing it in with your fingers until the mixture resembles coarse meal. Sprinkle the oat mixture evenly over the berries.

Bake until the berries are slightly bubbling and the top is crisp and golden brown, 40 to 45 minutes. Remove from the oven and cool on a wire rack.

Serve warm or at room temperature with vanilla ice cream.

Individual Nectarine Crisps with Crème Fraîche

SERVES 8

Crème fraîche may be store-bought, but I've included a recipe here nonetheless because I believe making it from scratch is a very rewarding enterprise. From the food-science perspective it's fascinating: a few ordinary ingredients set out at room temperature for a few days turn into another entity entirely. The sour crème adds a bit of contrast to the sweetness of the roasted nectarines, though you may wish to substitute whipped cream if you have a sweeter tooth. Use leftover crème fraîche to dollop on top of bowls of fresh berries or stir into soups.

4 tbsp/50 g unsalted butter

8 Amaretti (page 79), crushed

1 tsp grated zest
from 1 organic lemon

4 large nectarines, halved and pitted

2 tbsp honey

Crème Fraîche (recipe follows)

Heat the oven to 350°F/180°C. Lightly butter a medium baking dish.

Melt the butter in a saucepan, remove it from the heat, and cool. Stir in the crushed amaretti and lemon zest.

Arrange the nectarine halves in the baking dish, cut-side up. Spoon the amaretti mixture into the hollows of each nectarine half, filling each until the mixture is used up. Drizzle evenly with the honey.

Bake until the fruit is slightly tender and golden, 30 to 40 minutes. Remove the baking dish from the oven and rest for 1 hour.

Serve the crisps at room temperature with scoops of crème fraîche.

CRÈME FRAÎCHE

2 cups/480 ml heavy cream
1 cup/240 ml buttermilk

Place the cream and buttermilk in a large mason jar; stir. Let the mixture sit, uncovered, at room temperature for 24 to 48 hours until it thickens and begins to sour (the longer you leave it, the more sour it becomes). When it is sour enough for your taste, cover and store in the fridge until using.

Crème fraîche will keep in the fridge for up to 1 week.

Seasonal Fruit Tart with Coconut Cream

SERVES 12

Nut crusts can be a bit delicate to work with, so keep that in mind as you are assembling the base for this tart. (Fortunately it is pressed into the baking dish, which helps it keep its structure.) I like a combination of sliced strawberries and kiwis in season for the fruit layer, while blueberries dusted with a little lemon zest are very good as well. Soy or almond milk may be swapped in for the coconut milk.

NUT CRUST

10 oz/280 g nuts of choice,
such as almonds, hazelnuts, pecans,
or walnuts, or a combination

½ cup/30 g unsweetened flaked coconut

¼ cup/50 g sugar

¼ cup/60 ml oil of choice,
such as coconut, vegetable, or olive

COCONUT CREAM

¾ cup/150 g sugar

¼ tsp salt

½ cup/55 g cornstarch

3½ cups/840 ml coconut milk

¾ cup/180 ml water

1 tsp pure vanilla extract

1 lb/455 g (or more, if desired)
seasonal fruit, such as sliced pears and/or
apples, sliced strawberries and kiwis,
berries of choice, etc.

Lemon zest for serving (optional)

continued

Heat the oven to 350°F/180°C. Have a 9-in/23-cm pie plate or tart pan with a removable bottom ready.

To make the crust: Place the nuts and coconut in the bowl of a food processor fitted with a steel blade and process until finely ground. Pour into a large bowl and whisk in the sugar. Using a fork, gently cut in the oil until well combined (the nuts should hold together lightly when pinched). Press the crust evenly into the pan.

Bake until lightly and evenly browned, 10 to 12 minutes. Remove from the oven and cool completely on a wire rack before filling.

To make the cream: Place the sugar, salt, and cornstarch in a medium bowl and whisk together to combine. In a medium saucepan, heat the coconut milk until hot, but not boiling; remove from the heat. Gradually whisk the coconut milk into the cornstarch mixture; whisk in the water and vanilla. Cook the mixture over medium heat, stirring constantly, until it is thick and bubbling, about 10 minutes. Remove from the heat, place in a bowl, and cool to room temperature.

When ready to assemble, pour the cooled filling into the cooled crust and spread evenly with a spatula. Refrigerate for at least 4 hours.

Arrange the fresh fruit on top of the filling, scatter the lemon zest (if using) over the top, cut into wedges, and serve.

Plum Bake

SERVES 6

In this seasonal treat, plum slices are layered and drizzled with maple syrup and honey, sprinkled with mint and sliced nuts, and baked until the fruit is juicy, tender, and nearly melting—summer goodness on a plate. It's a simple enough dessert, but I love it for that: the plummy flavor of the fruit shines through and it's not overly sweet. Serve in generous portions with plain or Greek-style yogurt.

¼ cup/60 ml honey

¼ cup/60 ml maple syrup

2 tbsp warm water

2 lb/910 g plums, pitted and thinly sliced

10 fresh mint leaves, chopped

½ cup/50 g sliced almonds

Plain yogurt or vanilla ice cream
for serving

Heat the oven to 350°F/180°C. Lightly grease a medium baking dish with vegetable oil.

In a small bowl, whisk together the honey, maple syrup, and warm water until combined.

Place a layer of plum slices, slightly overlapping, on the bottom of the prepared baking dish. Top with one-third of the chopped mint and one-third of the almonds. Drizzle with some of the maple-honey syrup. Repeat until all of the plum slices, mint, and almonds are used up (you should be able to make three layers), finishing with the almonds. Drizzle the remaining maple-honey syrup over the top of the sliced almonds and plums.

Bake until the plums are slightly softened and syrup and juices are bubbling, 30 to 40 minutes. Remove from the oven and cool to room temperature on a wire rack.

Serve at room temperature or very slightly warm, with plain yogurt.

Baked Apples with Cinnamon Cream

SERVES 4

Baked apples are a wonderful transitional dessert in late summer to early fall to move the palate into the next season. They are also a lovely sweet finish to Thanksgiving dinner as an alternative to the ubiquitous pies sure to crowd the table. Use ground ginger in place of the cinnamon in the whipped cream to change things up every so often.

BAKED APPLES

4 large good baking apples,
such as Rome Beauty,
Golden Delicious, or Jonagold

4 tsp dried cranberries

2 tsp raisins

¼ cup/30 g chopped walnuts

2 tbsp unsalted butter,
at room temperature

2 tsp fresh lemon juice

2 tsp maple syrup

1 cup/240 ml apple cider or water

CINNAMON CREAM

1 cup/240 ml heavy cream

½ tsp ground cinnamon

Heat the oven to 375°F/190°C.

To make the apples: Using an apple corer or a paring knife, remove the apple cores to within about ½ in/12 mm of the bottom of the apples. Scrape out the seeds with a spoon and widen the holes until they are about ¾ in/2 cm to 1 in/2.5 cm wide.

In a small bowl, combine the cranberries, raisins, and chopped walnuts. Place the apples in an 8-by-8-in/20-by-20-cm square baking pan and stuff each apple with the dried fruit–nut mixture. Top each apple with a dot of butter. Drizzle the fresh lemon juice and maple syrup across the tops of the apples.

Pour the apple cider around the apples in the pan and place the pan in the oven. Bake until the apples are tender, but not mushy, 30 to 40 minutes. Remove from the oven and baste the apples several times with the pan juices.

To make the cream: In a large bowl, using an electric mixer, whip the cream and cinnamon together until soft peaks form.

Serve the apples warm or at room temperature, topped with dollops of cinnamon cream.

Spiced Poached Pears with Baked Vanilla Custard

SERVES 6

Pears poached in wine is a timeless classic that is also naturally flour-free. If you avoid alcohol, you can substitute water or apple juice for the wine with good results. Use pears that are not too ripe so that they do not disintegrate when cooked. Soy, almond, or coconut milk may be used in place of the 1½ cups/360 ml milk and 1 cup/240 ml cream (do a straight 2½ cups/600 ml substitution) if you are avoiding dairy. When you're pressed for time, serving the pears straight with a little whipped cream or vanilla ice cream (rather than the custard) makes for a nice alternative.

BAKED CUSTARD

1½ cups/360 ml whole milk

1 cup/240 ml heavy cream

1 vanilla bean, or 1 tsp pure vanilla extract

2 large eggs, plus 2 egg yolks

2 tbsp sugar

SPICED PEARS

1½ cups/360 ml dry white wine
or water

¼ cup/80 g honey

¼ tsp ground cinnamon or cardamom

6 firm pears,
peeled, cored, and halved

8 fresh mint leaves, slivered

½ cup/55 g shelled,
unsalted pistachio nuts,
chopped

Heat the oven to 350°F/180°C. Have six ½-cup/120-ml ramekins ready.

To make the custard: In a heavy saucepan, combine the milk and cream. Split the vanilla bean lengthwise and scrape the seeds into the milk mixture; add the pod (if using vanilla extract, stir in). Over medium heat, bring to just below boiling, then remove from the heat and let the mixture infuse for 15 minutes.

In a medium bowl, whisk together the eggs, egg yolks, and sugar. Remove and discard the vanilla pod from the milk mixture, and then slowly whisk the infused milk into the egg mixture until well combined.

Using a fine-mesh strainer, strain the custard evenly into each ramekin and set the ramekins in a roasting pan. Pour boiling water into the roasting pan until it reaches a little more than halfway up the sides of the ramekins. Carefully place the roasting pan in the oven and bake until the custards are set and no longer liquid, about 35 minutes.

Remove the roasting pan from the oven and transfer the custards to a wire rack to cool.

Chill the custards in the refrigerator until ready to serve. (Custards can be made up to 2 days in advance of serving.)

Meanwhile, to poach the pears: Combine the wine, honey, and ground cinnamon in a medium saucepan. Bring to a boil over medium heat, stirring occasionally until the honey melts.

Add the pear halves, decrease the heat to medium, and simmer gently, turning once, until the fruit is just tender but not falling apart, 2 to 5 minutes (watch that the fruit does not overcook). Place a lid on the pan, remove from the heat, and let stand to cool to room temperature. Transfer the pears and wine syrup to a bowl and refrigerate, covered with foil, for at least 8 hours to let the flavors meld.

Place a ramekin of vanilla custard on a dessert plate and place 2 pear halves alongside. Spoon some of the wine syrup over the pears. Garnish the pears with a sprinkling of the mint leaves and chopped pistachios to serve.

Roasted Stone Fruit with Honey Mascarpone and Mint

SERVES 6

In late summer, when stone fruit reaches its peak, not much is better than giving a clutch of your favorites a spate in the oven to bring out their inherent sweetness. Make this recipe with whatever stone fruit looks particularly good to you at your local market.

3 large, ripe peaches or nectarines, or 6 plums, halved and pitted

8 oz/225 g mascarpone cheese, at room temperature

¼ cup/80 g honey, plus more as needed

10 fresh mint leaves, slivered

Heat the oven to 350°F/180°C. Have a heatproof baking dish ready.

Place the fruit halves in the baking dish, cut-sides up. Bake until the fruit is slightly soft and has begun to release its juices a bit, about 30 minutes. Remove from the oven and set aside.

Meanwhile, in a large bowl, using an electric mixer, whip the mascarpone and honey on medium-high speed until well combined. Keep beating until the mixture is fluffy and creamy. Taste and add more honey, if desired.

Place a peach or nectarine half (or 2 plum halves) on a dessert plate. Put a generous dollop of mascarpone alongside the fruit and sprinkle the fruit with the slivered mint to serve.

Candies and Confections

Having a little stash of candy tucked away for impromptu nibbling is a guilty pleasure. I have simple tastes: a chunk of dried cranberry–laden dark chocolate to finish off lunch, a handful of caramel corn as a late-afternoon snack, or a piece of peanut brittle that doubles as an extra shot of protein. It's even better when the candy is homemade.

Making candy from scratch may seem intimidating but it's actually pretty easy (the secret is that making candy is not really that difficult or time-consuming). Nor does it call for expensive ingredients. And perhaps most important, it tastes so very good—far better, in my opinion, than the store-bought, overly sweet kind. An additional boon is that most of it is naturally flour-free.

Candy-making can be undertaken as a solitary pursuit on a chilly afternoon—mix up a pot of hot chocolate and settle comfortably into the kitchen—or with a group. The process involves a bit of science, a bit of ingenuity, and a bit of elbow grease. When it all comes together, it's a special kind of magic.

As the classic *Fannie Farmer Cookbook* so wisely puts it, "There is no reason except pure pleasure to make candy." And while the results surely bring about pure delight, the actual act of candy-creation is a soothing one. Sure, candy may not exactly be the benchmark of a healthful diet— and heaven knows there is enough corn syrup in the world—but we all need a treat every so often.

To that end, these recipes call neither for corn syrup nor flour but rely simply upon nuts, good chocolate, egg whites, sugar, and the occasional bit of butter to pull them together. Try giving the roasted and salted hazelnuts dusted with cocoa powder (see page 165) as gifts (if you can refrain from eating them all) as they keep very well, and tuck an assortment of Chocolate Truffles (page 164), Cranberry Fruit Jellies (page 170), and Pistachio-Coffee Toffee (page 176) into a holiday or birthday gift tin. (Save the Honey-Glazed Figs with Coffee Ice Cream, page 173, for your next dinner party.) The caramel corn (see page 179) you may hoard exclusively for yourself.

Chocolate Truffles

MAKES ABOUT 24 TRUFFLES

Think of chocolate truffles as a canvas onto which nearly anything can be incorporated: various nuts, ground spices such as cinnamon, dried fruit such as chopped dried cranberries, crystallized ginger, and more. This recipe is for a basic fail-safe truffle that needs no further improvements—it's hard to dislike chocolate melted with cream—but as you become more confident making it, try throwing in a few new flavors.

1¼ cups/300 ml heavy cream
9 oz/255 g good quality semisweet chocolate, chopped
Unsweetened cocoa powder for rolling

Line a baking sheet with parchment paper.

Bring the cream to a simmer over medium heat in a small heavy saucepan. Remove from the heat and cool to lukewarm, about 10 minutes.

Meanwhile, place the chocolate in a metal bowl set over a saucepan of simmering water and stir until the chocolate is melted and smooth. Remove from the heat and stir in the cream to make the truffle base.

Place the mixture in the refrigerator and chill the truffle base until it is firm enough to roll, about 3 hours.

Line a rimmed baking sheet with waxed paper. Scoop out 2 tsp of the truffle base and roll it between your palms to form a ball. Transfer to the prepared sheet. Repeat with the remaining truffle base. Chill until firm, about 1 hour.

When firm, gently roll each truffle ball in the cocoa powder.

Store in an airtight container in the fridge for up to 2 weeks.

TRUFFLE VARIATION

Don't roll the truffle balls in cocoa powder, but instead roll them in toasted, chopped nuts (or add a handful to the base), or dip in melted bittersweet chocolate. Let the truffles set in the fridge until firm before serving.

Cocoa-Dusted Salted Hazelnuts

MAKES ABOUT 6 CUPS/540 G NUTS

Here in San Francisco there's a wonderful chocolatier called Michael Recchiuti who makes all sorts of delectables such as s'mores bites, interesting little truffles and caramels, chocolate sauces, and to-die-for cocoa-dusted almonds that sparkle with crisp salt. These last are particularly special. I've sent packages of them to New England, brought them home to share in Sonoma County, and have even mailed some overseas if that gives you any indication of how good they are. I've come up with my own recipe that tastes quite similar; try any combination of nuts that suits your fancy, or stick to hazelnuts, per this recipe.

3 cups/350 g hazelnuts

½ cup/115 g unsalted butter,
cut into chunks

2 egg whites

1 cup/200 g sugar

1 tbsp unsweetened cocoa powder

1 tsp sea salt

Positon the rack in the center of the oven and heat the oven to 325°F/165°C.

Spread the hazelnuts evenly on a large baking sheet and toast in the oven until lightly browned, about 10 minutes. Remove from the oven, put them in a bowl, and set aside. (If your hazelnuts still have skins on, rub the nuts with your hands to loosen and remove any skin that might be ready to come off. Leaving the nuts with their skins on is perfectly acceptable, too.)

Scatter the butter over the baking sheet and place it in the oven for a few minutes to melt. As soon as the butter is melted, remove the baking sheet from the oven.

continued

In a large bowl, using an electric mixer, beat the egg whites on medium speed until they just start to hold their shape. Gradually add the sugar and continue to beat for 2 minutes. The whites will be sticky and glossy. (You will be making a meringue.)

Sift the cocoa powder over the beaten whites and gently fold in. Pour the cocoa mixture over the toasted nuts and fold together.

Spoon the coated nuts on top of the butter on the baking sheet in an even layer.

Bake, stirring the nuts after 10 minutes. After another 10 minutes, stir the nuts again (the meringue will be drying out a bit). Sprinkle the meringue-nut mixture with the salt; bake for 10 minutes more. Give it one last stir, breaking up the nuts a little, and bake until all the butter is absorbed and the nuts and coating are crisp, about 15 minutes.

Remove from the oven and place the pan on a wire rack to cool completely.

Store in an airtight container at room temperature for up to 1 week.

Bittersweet Chocolate Chunks with Dried Cranberries and Walnuts

MAKES ABOUT FORTY 1-IN/2.5-CM CUBES

These candies, which consist of semisweet chocolate melted and poured over chopped nuts and dried cranberries, are difficult to resist. A little chewy from the fruit and a bit crunchy from the nuts, these chocolate chunks are one of my most favorite homemade candies to date.

2/3 cup/80 g shelled pistachios, salted or unsalted

2/3 cup/85 g walnuts

1¼ lb/570 g good-quality semisweet chocolate, finely chopped

1 cup/80 g dried cranberries, chopped

Heat the oven to 350°F/180°C. Line the bottom and sides of an 8-in/23-cm square baking pan with aluminum foil, leaving a 2-in/5-cm overhang. Lightly brush the foil with vegetable oil.

Spread the pistachios and walnuts out on a rimmed baking sheet. Place in the oven and toast the nuts until they are lightly browned, about 10 minutes. Remove the baking sheet from the oven and let the nuts cool completely, then turn out onto a cutting board and coarsely chop.

In the top of a double boiler or a metal bowl set over a saucepan of barely simmering water, melt the chocolate, stirring until smooth.

When the chocolate has melted, remove it from the heat and stir in the chopped fruit and nuts. Pour the mixture into the prepared pan and spread it evenly with a rubber spatula. Place the pan in the refrigerator and chill until the chocolate is firm, but not rock hard, about 1 hour (if it gets rock hard, the chocolate will shatter when cut). Let the chocolate warm up very slightly at room temperature before cutting, if necessary.

Using the foil overhang, lift the chilled chocolate mixture from the pan and place it on a cutting board. Remove the foil and cut the chocolate into 1-in/2.5-cm pieces.

Store in an airtight container in the fridge for up to 2 weeks.

Cranberry Fruit Jellies

MAKES ABOUT 36 CANDIES

Using pectin (rather than gelatin) makes these jellies perfectly suitable for the vegetarian candy eater. Dusting with sugar after the jellies are cut makes them sparkle—perfect for the holidays, especially when using seasonal fruit. As you become more comfortable making this recipe, try other fruits in place of the cranberries such as oranges or clementines, substituting 2 cups/480 ml fruit for the cranberries (reduce the water to ½ cup/120 ml) and adding it with the pears.

1½ lb/680 g firm-ripe Bartlett pears
cored and quartered (peel left on)

One 12-oz/340-g bag fresh
or frozen cranberries

1 cup/240 ml water

4 cups/800 g sugar

2 tbsp unsalted butter

1 tsp grated fresh ginger

Two 3-oz/85-g packages liquid pectin

Line the bottom and sides of an 8-by-8-in/20-by-20-cm pan with plastic wrap, pressing flat into the bottom and corners of the pan.

Cut the pears into ½-in/12-mm pieces. Place the pears, cranberries, water, 3¾ cups/750 g of the sugar, the butter, and ginger in a large, heavy pot and bring to a boil over moderately high heat, stirring occasionally. Decrease the heat to low and simmer, covered, stirring occasionally, until the cranberries burst and the pears are tender, about 10 minutes.

Carefully transfer the hot mixture to the bowl of a food processor fitted with a steel blade and puree until smooth, about 1 minute. Force the mixture through a medium-mesh sieve back into the pot, pressing on the solids with back of a spoon to get out as much liquid as possible. Discard the solids.

Put a plate in the freezer to chill.

Bring the cranberry mixture to a boil over high heat and add the pectin. Decrease the heat to medium and cook, stirring frequently, until it is very thick and paste-like, about 45 minutes.

To test for doneness, remove the pot from the heat and drop 1 tsp of the cranberry mixture on the chilled plate and chill in the freezer for 1 minute. Tilt the plate; the mixture should remain in a firm mound and not run. If the mixture runs, continue cooking and stirring, and repeat the test every 5 minutes.

When the mixture has reached the desired stage, remove it from the heat and immediately pour it into the prepared pan. Gently tap the sides of pan to smooth the top and eliminate any air bubbles.

Cool to room temperature at least 1 hour, then cover the surface directly with plastic wrap and chill until firm, at least 2 hours.

Cut into small squares in the pan, or use small cookie cutters to cut into other shapes. Roll in or dust with the remaining ¼ cup/50 g sugar.

Store in an airtight container in the fridge for up to 2 weeks.

Honey-Glazed Figs with Coffee Ice Cream

SERVES 4

Figs have two seasons: a quick, short season in early summer, and a second, longer one that starts in late summer and runs through the fall. Take advantage of them while they're plentiful; this dessert really allows the unique flavor of fresh figs to shine through. You can save a lot of time by using store-bought ice cream here, of course, but it's awfully nice to make your own. The ice cream needs time to freeze up, so you can make it hours to a whole day ahead. The figs come together in minutes. Another time, serve the figs with scoops of Crème Fraîche (page 151) or tangy Greek yogurt.

COFFEE ICE CREAM

1½ cups/360 ml whole milk

¾ cup/150 g sugar

1½ cups/170 g whole coffee beans

⅛ tsp salt

1½ cups/360 ml heavy cream

5 egg yolks

¼ tsp pure vanilla extract

¼ tsp finely ground coffee

HONEY-GLAZED FIGS

12 fresh figs, any local variety, halved and tops trimmed

3 tbsp honey

To make the ice cream: In a medium saucepan, heat the milk, sugar, coffee beans, salt, and ½ cup/120 mL of the cream until warm, but not boiling. Remove from the heat, cover, and let steep at room temperature for 1 hour.

continued

Set a medium metal bowl over a larger bowl of ice and pour in the remaining 1 cup/240 ml cream. Place a fine-mesh strainer on top of the metal bowl. Set aside.

Warm the milk-coffee mixture over medium heat. In a separate bowl, whisk the egg yolks. Slowly pour the heated milk-coffee mixture into the egg yolks, whisking constantly so that the egg yolks don't cook. Scrape the warmed mixture back into the saucepan.

Stir the mixture constantly over medium heat with a rubber spatula, scraping the bottom as you stir, until it thickens and coats the spatula, about 10 minutes.

Pour the custard through the strainer into the cream and stir the mixture to blend. Press the coffee beans into the strainer to extract as much of the coffee flavor as possible; discard the beans. Mix in the vanilla and finely ground coffee and stir until the mixture is cool.

Chill the mixture thoroughly in the refrigerator, then freeze it in your ice-cream maker according to the manufacturer's instructions.

To make the figs: Position the rack in the center of the oven and heat the broiler to high. Line a baking sheet with aluminum foil. Gently squeeze the fig halves to remove their skins.

Place the fig halves on the foil-lined baking sheet and drizzle the figs with the honey. Broil the figs for 5 minutes, then remove from the oven.

Serve the figs warm with scoops of the ice cream.

Peanut-Sesame Brittle

MAKES ABOUT 24 CANDIES

While the sugar in these delicate little candies saves them from being entirely too healthful, they are nonetheless chock-full of protein in the form of peanuts and sesame seeds. You may also substitute an equivalent amount of almonds for the peanuts, or try sunflower seeds in place of the sesame seeds.

2 cups/260 g raw unsalted peanuts

½ cup/60 g sesame seeds

1 cup/200 g packed
light or dark brown sugar

½ tsp salt

2 egg whites

Heat the oven to 350°F/180°C. Line a baking sheet with parchment paper.

In a large bowl, stir together the peanuts, sesame seeds, brown sugar, and salt. In another large bowl, using an electric mixer, beat the egg whites on medium-high speed until they form soft peaks.

Stir about half the whites into the nut mixture, then fold in the remaining whites, stirring to gently incorporate all of the whites.

Spread the mixture evenly on the prepared baking sheet. Bake until the brittle turns light brown, about 25 minutes. Remove from the oven and place on a wire rack to cool; remove the parchment paper while the brittle is still a bit warm.

Allow the brittle to cool and harden completely before breaking it into small squares.

Store in an airtight container in the fridge for up to 2 weeks.

Pistachio-Coffee Toffee

MAKES ABOUT 2 LB/910 G TOFFEE

I came up with this toffee variation, a favorite around the holidays or anytime, because I was feeling especially nostalgic for Greece— and, to me, coffee and pistachios are so evocative of that place. Even in December, a piece of this candy reminds me of sipping hot, strong coffee and nibbling homegrown pistachios while looking out over the Mediterranean on a late summer afternoon. It's best to make toffee on a cooler day, as heat and humidity can affect its ability to harden.

2 cups/220 g shelled
pistachio nuts

1 cup/200 g granulated sugar

⅓ cup/65 g packed brown sugar

2 tsp instant espresso powder

½ tsp ground cinnamon

⅓ cup/75 ml water

1 tbsp dark unsulfured molasses

1 cup/225 g unsalted butter

4½ oz/130 g semisweet chocolate,
finely chopped

4½ oz/130 g milk chocolate,
finely chopped

Heat the oven to 325°F/165°C. Have an ungreased baking sheet and a buttered rimmed baking sheet or jelly-roll pan ready.

Spread the pistachios on the ungreased baking sheet and toast in the oven until they are fragrant, 5 to 10 minutes (watch so they do not burn). Remove from the oven and cool for 10 minutes. Coarsely chop and put in a bowl.

In a medium bowl, combine both sugars, the espresso powder, and cinnamon. In another small bowl or measuring cup, whisk together the water and molasses.

Melt the butter in a heavy 2½-qt/2-L saucepan over low heat.

Add the sugar-espresso and water-molasses mixtures to the saucepan and stir until the sugars dissolve.

Increase the heat to medium and cook until the mixture registers 290°F/140°C on a candy thermometer, stirring occasionally and scraping the bottom of the pan, about 15 minutes.

Remove the pan from the heat and quickly stir in 1½ cups/165 g of the nuts. Immediately pour the mixture onto the buttered baking sheet. With a spatula, spread the toffee to a ¼-in/6-mm thickness. Sprinkle the chocolate by generous tablespoonfuls atop the toffee, alternating bittersweet and milk chocolates. Let stand for 1 minute to melt the chocolate. Using the back of a spoon or a spatula, spread the melted chocolate slightly to coat the toffee. Sprinkle with the remaining ½ cup/55 g chopped nuts.

Refrigerate on the pan, uncovered, until the toffee is firm, about 1 hour. With a sharp knife, slice the toffee evenly or break into rough pieces.

Store in an airtight container in the fridge for up to 2 weeks.

Sweet-Salty Caramel Corn

SERVES 12

San Francisco's Miette Bakery sells delicious packets of caramel corn out of their bayside Ferry Building store. As I was nearly bankrupting myself every time I went by there, I finally decided to try my own version. This recipe perfectly fulfills my penchant for the sweet-salty, is surprisingly easy to put together, and can be made vegan with the substitution of nondairy margarine for the butter. (If you prefer a less salty corn, omit 1 tsp of the salt.) Make a little extra popcorn to snack on while you have a batch in the oven.

10 cups/142 g freshly popped popcorn
(about ¾ cup/115 g unpopped corn)

6 tbsp/85 unsalted butter or nondairy margarine,
such as Earth Balance

1 cup/200 packed
light or dark brown sugar

¼ cup/60 ml maple syrup

Heaping 1½ tsp salt

2 tbsp water

½ tsp baking soda

2 tsp pure vanilla extract

1 cup/130 g unsalted peanuts

Heat the oven to 250°F/120°C. Line a rimmed baking sheet with parchment paper.

Oil a large bowl and dump in the popped popcorn.

In a medium saucepan, melt the butter. Whisk in the brown sugar, maple syrup, salt, and water. Bring to a simmer over medium-high heat. Continue to simmer, whisking often, until the mixture registers 250°F/120°C on a candy thermometer, 3 to 4 minutes. Immediately remove the pan from the heat and whisk in the baking soda and vanilla. Quickly pour the hot caramel over the popcorn.

continued

Using a rubber spatula, gently fold the caramel into the popcorn, stirring to distribute it evenly. Stir in the peanuts and transfer the mixture to the prepared baking sheet. Bake for 1 hour, stirring and turning the popcorn with a spatula every 20 minutes or so.

Remove the pan from the oven and cool on a wire rack for 20 minutes. Gently break up the popcorn into pieces and serve.

Store in an airtight container at room temperature for up to 1 week.

Acknowledgments

This cookbook grew out of a conversation in a Maine kitchen during the cold, dark heart of a January night while my sister-in-law and I munched on peanut butter cookies and discussed flourless baking. From that inkling of an idea and throughout the recipe developing and testing that followed, I have had a solid support base that has carried me through many solitary hours working in my small kitchen. I may have seemed alone in front of my oven as I worked, but in truth I was not, and I am ever grateful. Many thanks go to:

My cadre of faithful recipe testers (and tasters): Emily Dittmann, Lesli Frederick, Lisa Horvath Chase, Kat and Soren Ogden, Lupe Rodriguez, and Helen Spiridakis. Thank you for your good will, copious notes, and enthusiasm. My apologies for any weight gained during the process.

The editors I have worked with throughout my journalism career, in particular Bonny Wolf and John C. Abell. Thank you for your keen eyes and for making me a better writer every day.

The San Francisco office of the U.S. Commercial Service. Thank you for consuming all the treats presented to you, and for your thoughtful commentary. Without you I might still be buried under a pile of cookies.

All the friends invited over for dinner and whom I have pressed into service as inadvertent taste testers. You know who you are. Thank you for letting me ply you with my experiments. I truly appreciate each and every one of you.

My parents, Nick and Helen Spiridakis, for eating (nearly) everything I serve them—and seeming to like it!—and for their unflagging support of all of my endeavors throughout the years. And to my brother, Kurt Spiridakis, who inspires me in and out of the kitchen and reminds me often to "keep it real." Thank you for being in my life.

My sister-in-law, Emily Dittmann, for providing the impetus and the idea for this cookbook. Thank you for the ongoing conversation. I have learned, and continue to learn, so much.

My husband—and oldest friend—Doug Wallace. Thank you for cheering me along in the face of the occasional baking disaster, providing me with an oven thermometer at a critical moment, for taste-testing "just one bite!" of every single recipe produced during the making of this book, for the many cups of tea, and for your unconditional support and kindness. I love you.

And to Sierra, who was with me all the way.

Index